TEENAGE MUTANT *NINJA* TURTLES
EXPOSED!

JOAN HAKE ROBIE

TEENAGE MUTANT *NINJA* TURTLES *EXPOSED!*

JOAN HAKE ROBIE

STARBURST PUBLISHERS

P.O. Box 4123, Lancaster, Pennsylvania 17604

JOAN HAKE ROBIE, author of thirteen books, which include *Horror and Violence—The Deadly Duo In The Media, Turmoil In The Toy Box II*, and *Reverse The Curse In Your Life*, now brings you this critical analysis—*Teenage Mutant Ninja Turtles Exposed*! Joan has appeared on TV shows such as Geraldo Rivera, Sonya Live in L.A., People Are Talking, and Heritage Today. She has been a regular guest on The Morton Downey Jr. Show. Joan conducts seminars throughout the country bringing up-to-date information on the toy and cartoon industry, the occult, and other timely subjects.

To schedule Author appearances write: Author Appearances, Starburst Promotions, P.O. Box 4123, Lancaster, PA 17604 or call (717)-293-0939.

Credits:

Cover Art by Dave Ivey.
Editorial Assistance by Linda Straitiff.

TEENAGE MUTANT NINJA TURTLES EXPOSED!

First Printing, March 1991

Revised Edition:
First Printing, September 1991

ISBN: 0-914984-31-4
Library of Congress Catalog Number 91-66361

Printed in the United States of America

Contents

Preface

Teenage Mutant Ninja Turtles are called "the world's most fiercesome fighting teens." The word "mutant" (Teenage Mutant Ninja Turtles), means—having to do with or undergoing mutation (an animal or plant with inheritable characteristics that differ from those of the parents).

Some of the ways that Teenage Mutant Ninja Turtles are different from ordinary turtles are : they are giant-sized, they are green in color, they talk, and they are skilled in the Ninja Arts (a deadly art that I will discuss later in this book).

This book reveals, among other things: who the Teenage Mutant Ninja Turtles are, why they are so popular, their philosophy and how it is affecting our children, and what we can do about it.

Whether by title of this book, or artist rendition of the Turtles, or others, or the name Teenage Mutant Ninja Turtles, or whatsoever, this book, or its cover, or its contents, is in no way intended to "cause confusion, or to cause mistake, or to deceive" either the public, or the creators, copyright holders, patent holders, etc., of the registered trademark or logo of Teenage Mutant Ninja Turtles.

This book has been written solely for the purpose of "critical analysis" only, due to the many requests for same from the parents and others who hate violence and are interested in the well-being of their children.

1

What Are The Teenage Mutant Ninja Turtles?

Teenage Mutant Ninja Turtles
Teenage Mutant Ninja Turtles
Teenage Mutant Ninja Turtles
Heroes in a half-shell;
Turtle power!

They're the world's most fiercesome fighting teens.
We're really hip!
They're heroes in the half-shell and they're green.
Hey, we're the greatest!
When the evil Shredder attacks . . .
These turtle boys don't cut him no slack.

Teenage Mutant Ninja Turtles
Teenage Mutant Ninja Turtles

Splinter taught them to be ninja teens.
He's a radical rat!
Leonardo leads; Donatello does machines.
That's a fact. Jack!
Raphael is cool but rude; Michaelangelo is a party dude.

Teenage Mutant Ninja Turtles
Teenage Mutant Ninja Turtles
Teenage Mutant Ninja Turtles
Heroes in a half-shell;
Turtle Power!

"Please, Mommy," begged little Bobby as he quickly pulled a Teenage Mutant Ninja Turtle action figure named Donatello down from the toy shelf, "all the kids have them. I gotta have a Turtle too. They're so 'cool!' "

This scene is being repeated throughout this country and abroad as children are being encouraged via the television and the toy store to "run out and buy" everything from a Sewer Seltzer Cannon (which squirts water) to a Mutant Killer Bee.

Why all the fuss about Teenage Mutant Ninja Turtles? Where did they come from? Let's find out!

The Teenage Mutant Ninja Turtles were born in 1983, out of the febrile imaginations of two unknown illustrators, Kevin Eastman, now 27, and Peter Laird, 36. Laird had been "scraping out a living" drawing eggplants and such for the gardening page of a newspaper in Massachusetts when the editor of a local comic magazine suggested that he collaborate with Eastman, an amateur cartoonist who was working as a short-order cook. **Late one night, the story goes, inspiration struck. Eastman drew a human-sized turtle wearing a ninja mask and carrying a katana blade. The idea of a slowpokey turtle as a swift and wily ninja**

cracked them up. By the end of the evening, they had trash-compacted the outstanding features of mainstream comic superheroes into a half-spoof, half-serious tale of a bright rat named Splinter.

Many years ago in Japan, Splinter was the pet of Yoshi, an honorable ninja master (ninja are super-samurai, possessing a potent combination of martial arts skills and spiritual and magical powers). Yoshi was forced to flee to New York with his girlfriend where both were murdered by his archrival from Japan, a Darth Vader-like masked man named Shredder.

After permanently scarring the bad guy, Splinter escaped into the sewers of Manhattan. Then a street accident sloshed a container of radioactive waste—and four baby turtles—into his lair. The blob of "retromutogenic" slime turns the turtles into turtle-style adolescents, complete with a passion for pizza and banter borrowed from black and chicano cultures.

In saving the baby turtles, Splinter himself became radioactive and suddenly grew to a human-sized ninja master with superhuman intelligence. He took the more slowly-evolving turtles under his wing, naming them after Renaissance artists (Donatello, Raphael, Michaelangelo and Leonardo). He instructed them in martial arts and philosophy while they educated themselves in the folkways of human teenagers by creeping out at night, disguised in raincoats and fedoras. The Turtles are capable of great feats, but to the exasperation of "Master Splinter," behave rather irresponsibly as soon as they are off duty.

As their saga opened in the comic books, the Turtles fought Shredder and his evil Foot Clan above ground, or hung out in their sewer home, drinking beer and eating pizza in humongous quantities. This combination of street talk, pizzaphilia, martial arts and a vague gesture towards global

11

ecological catastrophe is a pretty zany concept, and the creators failed to sell their original concept to the major comic book publishing houses. So, in 1983 the Turtles' inventors finally published their comic themselves—for the adult and teenage market rather than children. It became a cult success, leading to some custom made spin-off items.

For five years the first Turtle comics achieved a respectable following among 150,000 teenagers and young adult comic-book collectors. The real Turtle explosion began in 1986 when a deal was made with Mark Freedman, a canny licensing agent. He convinced a California company, Playmates, to invest $2.5 million in an animated television show and launch a line of ten figures. With his encouragement Archie Comic Publications printed 550,000 monthly of a Ninja Turtle comic book.

Merchandisers adapted the Turtle "concept" for an audience of four to ten year-olds, simplifying and multiplying the format into a cartoon series and emphasizing the science-fiction elements. Unfortunately, the tendency for punks and villains on the show to fall into racial stereotypes also emerged. The response was staggering and by 1988 there were over 600 Turtle products aimed squarely at the booming kiddie market. This included a line of action toys and a Nintendo game that toy stores cannot keep on the shelves. In the widely popular Archie comics and the television version six-packs of beer are eliminated, but pizza, California surfer-speak and humor are all big. Legions of grownups are finding themselves surrounded by little people in green suits brandishing plastic martial-arts weapons and screaming "Turtle Power!" and "Cowabunga" (the latter war cry was borrowed from Howdy Doody's chief Thunderthud). Children are throwing tantrums in front of Turtle toy stands, begging parents to buy yet another item. The question, of course is why? **Why should a goofy tale of turtles trained in the martial-arts by the most distasteful father figure,** an oversized rodent with matted fur, bleary eyes and a Zen-like aura hold such an attraction for America's—indeed, the world's—teen and under crowd?

MICHAELANGELO

2

Why Are
The Turtles So Popular?

While most parents can't fathom their appeal, most kids under fourteen love the Turtles' cool lingo, slithery look and jovial personalities. They also flip for the way the agile critters bound about despite their clunky shells. Robert Shayne, chairman of New Line, says that the Turtles play to the kids' rebellious streak, "They're iconoclastic, straight-talking, fantasy characters. They appeal to the kids precisely because adults don't understand them."[1]

"They took the seriousness out of superheroes and brought wackiness and zaniness in," says Playmates Executive Vice President of Marketing, Richard Sallis. "Far from displaying superhuman sternness, the Ninja Turtles, like human teenagers, squabble with their siblings, live for pizza, understand life through TV, and fawn somewhat crudely over unattainable babes."[2]

Kids adore their hip and slightly naughty sense of humor: "Let's haul shell out of here." Their jokes are campy, the ninja feats daring, and the Turtles (like human brothers) squabble noisily over practically everything.

The Teenage Mutant Ninja Turtles have been a huge market success, so much so that Surge Licensing can hardly keep up with the applications to produce Turtle-related objects.

"They are just flying off the shelves," said David Valentine, a toy industry analyst for Standard & Poors. Valentine considers the turtles to be the natural descendants of the tin soldier with appealingly distasteful roots in radioactive gunk. "Kids are into slime," he said. "Anything to gross out their little sisters."[3]

These toys enable children (especially boys) to re-enact scenarios of masculine bonding and fighting. This popularity is closely linked to that of Thundercats or Ghostbusters. Like Ghostbusters, the Turtles are a bunch of do-gooding guys, wisecracking their way to victory with an obligatory woman in tow. The Ghostbusters had Janine, their secretary; the Turtles have an ally in a woman TV reporter. Team spirit, jokes and a superficial show of incompetence predominate. However, the Turtles seem to have a fascination for adults, too: a layer of references and jokes which adults can see but children usually cannot. This caused some marketing problems with the Turtles' movie. Jonathan Rutter, publicity agent pointed out, "We are very anxious to separate the cartoon from the film. Obviously we hope that the film can be enjoyed by the very young but we have a different target audience of teenagers and young adults."[4]

This is precisely one problem with the Turtles. Aside from the fact that it deals with a culture the children know little or nothing about, it is technically impossible to appeal to widely opposing markets. The level of sophistication of humor for a four year-old is vastly different than that of a teenager. The Turtles, by trying to reach both audiences does a disservice to the young viewers. In addition, parents who have consistently permitted their children to watch the cartoon series have no reason to think that the movie will be any different.

The Teenage Mutant Ninja Turtles appeal to the young audience because of its "realism." This is an apparent paradox for such a bizarre series, but the Turtles reflect back to their audience a strong and prevalent image of the streetwise gang. This is then integrated into the predictable format of good versus evil, where the motiveless and arbitrary struggle between two forces provides the backdrop for a kind of fantasy vigilanteism that currently seems such a vital part of the fantasy of boys. But the Turtles seem to appeal to the girls too in a way that previous cartoons of this type have not. This might be because the Turtles are less excluding than soldiers, or because the martial arts, based on skill rather than brute strength, have always held some fascination for girls. **"Before I saw the movie, I thought Teenage Mutant Ninja Turtles were stupid roly-poly things," said Heather Doherty, age 11. "Now I know they are totally awesome dudes. Teenage Mutant Ninja Turtles aren't just for boys anymore. They're fun and sensitive and aren't like G.I. Joe and the Hulk. The movie isn't that violent; still it's not Cinderella and you probably shouldn't take your little babies."**[5]

Mark Freedman says of the Turtles, "They have a sense of humor. They're like the Bruce Willis character in 'Moonlighting.' They talk directly to the audience, and they don't take themselves too seriously. Another draw is that parents don't get it."[6]

3

An "Innocent" Fairy Tale?

Although shrewd showmanship alone may explain the success of the Teenage Mutant Ninja Turtles, their drawing power also comes from their capturing the elementary needs and anxieties of childhood fairy tales.

A fairy tale is defined by experts as "constructing a universe where literally everything can change and anything can happen; where the extraordinary is made to seem quite ordinary."[7] Simply and persuasively, a tale speaks to the child's existential helplessness and then offers homely reassurance. Its typical hero has been agonizingly abandoned, cast out or separated from the shelter of home and family. Whether due to evil or accident, the child dwells in dark, lonely surroundings until help arrives through the agency of a benevolent, magical "other," frequently an animal.

How can a turtle fit into the fairy tale universe? While the animal is actually well-adapted for survival, the turtle is usually seen by children as a cute, pokey creature with very limited means of defense, and even less inclination towards attack. The Turtle heroes are delivered as extremely vulnerable infants into the dark world of the scary sewer. Here they would surely perish if it weren't for the mutated Splinter's prompt rescue. Children generally recognize this as fanciful business, but also seem to think that such occurrences aren't particularly surprising in a world of spaceships and atomic energy.

The traditional fairy tale not only acknowledges its listeners' yearning for healthy dependency, but also affirms their desire for independence from parental guidance. It tells children that they are worthwhile, then tutors them in the belief that with persistence and courage, their own skills in coping with life's tasks will surely ripen.

In the cast of the Ninja Turtles, "magical" radiation matures them toward human form and competence. But the progress is helped by Splinter's wisdom, his repeated admonition to stand on one's own two-toed feet, and practice, practice, practice—whether at swordplay or the mastery of unruly feelings. Although his "sons" have learned much as their story begins, they are still small relative to the size and menace of their enemies—a point of further identification for young viewers.

Fairy tale characters are portrayed as either all good or all evil. This polarization conveniently taps into the child's natural tendency to externalize negative aspects (real or imagined) of its parents as well as unacceptable inner feelings such as anger, jealously, etc. In the case of the fairy tale, children project their "bad" feelings upon an unabashedly bad villain whose destruction is totally justified within the tale's context: a wolf, a wicked step-mother—or a Shredder.

No matter how exceptional a fairy tale's scenario, children

value its inevitable return to reality. Much of the Turtles' fascination does indeed appear related to a welcome ordinariness of their behavior and language, belying their strange appearance. The verbal fencing, put-downs and puns that adults find "just plain dumb" are hilariously familiar to children. They also identify with their idols' sloppy orality, their passion for junk food, the slovenly comforts and secrecy of their underground clubhouse.

The Turtles are latchkey kids with a vengence. The father in charge serves up a portion of Zen-like advice that sounds like Rambo macho. The consolation embodied in a traditional fairy tale is never available through the Turtles, since every Turtle story ends with a temporary triumph over Shredder and his vile pals. That is, until the unthinking pummeling starts anew next time around.

"Some might believe that the little boys who comprise the Turtles' main audience need a safe release in fantasy for their native pugnacious tendencies and that our (Turtle) heroes answer this need. Any assumption that little boys might have inborn aggression must be controversial. But even assuming that some need for release does exist in little boys, must there be so much combat in the Turtles' scenarios, with half of humanity excluded, and so little available in constructive nurturing except pepperoni pizza?"[8]

RAPHAEL

4

The Turtles As Movie Stars

The Teenage Mutant Ninja Turtles are the subjects of a monstrously successful movie. The film featuring live versions of these wisecracking, sword-wielding, pizza-gobbling little characters immediately broke all box office records by pulling in more than $25 million in its first weekend in theaters. It then went on to earn $114,032,497 in its first 52 days of presenting its brand of violent teenage cheeky humor in American theaters.

The film targets adolescent sensibilities and themes, but the advertising seems to aim beyond teenagers to the small children who make up the Turtles' greatest constituency.

In the midst of the hype, experts and many parents are beginning to worry about possible harmful effects (especially on the very young children) of viewing the movie's unrelenting karate-chopping and related mayhem. Seven year-old Peter Russell was asked his opinion of the Turtles' movie, "It was kind of rough but I wasn't scared. The best part was when the Turtles were fighting the Foot Clan in the fire. Leonardo threw his sword at a light bulb, it broke and everybody was fighting. Only one person got killed. Everybody got jumped."[9] Even a seven year-old can recognize the extreme amount of violence contained in this movie.

The value placed on combat as the main solution to life's problems as well as the avalanche of commercialism accompanying the film are cause for worry. Newsweek magazine asked eleven year-old David Kaye to review the movie. He said, "One major point that the movie lacks is originality. I felt a slight Three Musketeers likeness in the way the Turtles fought: all for one and one for all. Star Wars was mixed in the movie, too, with Shredder having almost all the characteristics of Darth Vader. Overall, I would say it was fairly enjoyable, but mainly a publicity stunt to boost Ninja Turtle sales."[10]

Another question raised is whether the live action of the film may overwhelm young viewers who are no longer watching make-believe cartoon characters but see the Turtles as real and their adventure as reality.

In recent years action-oriented children's television cartoons such as "G.I. Joe" have become stripped of narrative interest and quality in favor of endless violence. Today's shows present a polarized, vacant "us versus them" world with no shades of gray to an ever-younger audience. Noise has increasingly replaced artistic sophistication. The problem is that for young children the boundary between reality and fantasy is not always clear.

The Movie's Storyline

When the movie opens, New York City is in the grip of a terrible crime wave. There are thefts of everything from stereos to skateboards. The perpetrators are latchkey kids befriended, brainwashed, then trained for a life of crime by

Shredder, an evil crime lord, a martial arts expert who has a heavy Japanese accent and operates a disco-like den of iniquity. There, after a long day of thievery, the lost boys gross out on video games, pool, poker, soft drinks, and the forbidden cigarette.

Because the Manhattan police are so dimwitted, the job of saving the city falls to a pretty television newscaster named April, a young man named Casey Jones, the wise old Splinter and the Turtles.

" 'Teenage Mutant Ninja Turtles' breaks a lot of rules," says New York Times reviewer Vincent Canby. "Japanese myths have been effortlessly integrated into our pop culture."[11]

Much of the story takes place at night, therefore the movie is exceptionally dark for a childrens' film. Yet, the sewer home of Splinter and his ninja students has the cozy atmosphere of a kids' clubhouse furnished with stuff discarded by others: a moth-eaten sofa, an ancient television set, a pay-telephone and an easy chair where Splinter sits and instructs his charges in truth, karate, beauty, patience and meditation.

Shredder kidnaps Splinter, who in turn convinces one latchkey youth into converting to the Turtles' cause and rejoining his divorced father. The Turtles are aided in their rescue of Splinter by April O'Neil, a reporter who is their chief contact with the above-sewer work. There is much mayhem in the movie as the Turtles take on platoons of lost boys and the members of Shredder's armed household guard, the Foot Clan. However, they and Splinter handily dispose of Shredder. The lost boys see the error of their ways and all is made right.

Too Alive?

The hurtfulness of the Teenage Mutant Ninja Turtles movie for very small children is a significant concern. The comic strip frame by virtue of its stillness on the page offers a flatness and compression. These often don't translate well into three dimensions with the result being that a "live" movie seems somehow less real than the animated version. The reverse phenomenon may very well operate for the young viewers of the Turtle movie. They can easily process their heroes' aggression, if it is contained by the printed page or small screen. However, the cinematic Turtles are literally five feet tall, exuberantly three-dimensional and more than a bit intimidating. Splinter's rattiness seems unexpectedly repelling.

While no heads are chopped off, the movie's fight scenes proceed almost nonstop against a background of an overmiked soundtrack. Many of the children watching the movie seem overwhelmed. The film also strongly addresses the emotional issues of the teen-age years. The mutation theme is put in service of the search of a viable identity and bridging the generation gap is stressed relentlessly. Endless references to other movies and television programs abound.

Critical opinions of "Teenage Mutant Ninja Turtles" has been almost uniformly negative, but critics don't count much against the pull of a fad like the Turtles.

The Director

"If you took away the ninja aspect," said Steve Barron in reference to the extreme violence in 'Teenage Mutant Ninja Turtles,' "it would be like taking away the swords from the Three Musketeers . . . you're looking at an interpretation of an existing phenomenon that I don't think could have been done any other way."[12] He prefers to describe the film as a fantasy movie for a family audience.

If one takes a hard look at the Turtles' movie, it is easy to recognize that the director of the film, Steve Barron, is best noted for his rock music videos. Mr. Barron is a founder (in 1980) and partner with Simon Fields in Limelight Films, a company associated with rock music videos. Mr. Barron's background as a director includes the feature film "Electric Dreams," several episodes of the NBC series "Storyteller," and the award-winning video of "Billie Jean" from Michael Jackson's "Thriller."

Steve Barron was approached by Tom Gray, the president of Golden Harvest Films, in November 1988 about directing the film. The project was described to him as doing a bizarre comic book, and bizarre it was. "The ideas from the early comic books were very strong, very clever—the ideas behind the names, the characterizations, the background story of the turtles, the way they came to be, the villains," he said. "I talked to Simon Fields . . . . We both read the comics and thought: How can we do this? The way to do this would be through animatronics. It's robotics, creature-related robotics."[13]

Mr. Barron's next move was to call Jim Henson, creator of the Muppets to see if his London-based Creature Shop experts had the proper technology to create walking, talking, leaping turtles. "Animatronics are quite common," he said, "but they are rarely attempted in a short space of time. We had only twelve weeks in which to design, build and develop the turtles. You had 17 functions articulating faces from the eyebrow to the jaw. They all had to be articulated by puppeteers," he said of the complicity of the Turtles' radio-controlled heads.[14] The main concern was to make the film quickly, while popularity of the ninja turtles was strong.

The Producer

It is not surprising to find that the production offices of the company producing "Teenage Mutant Ninja Turtles" are in a building whose entrance is marked by a flower-bedecked Buddhist shrine. Nor is it difficult to guess that Raymond Chow, owner of Golden Harvest

29

International is the man who discovered and profited from the talent of Bruce Lee and Jackie Chan, two karate-chopping film stars. Kung-fu movies have been making this man immensely rich for the past 20 years. These movies have lots of action, can be produced cheaply, have international appeal, and sequels can be concocted fairly easily. Mr. Chow recognized these qualities in the Turtles movie after virtually every major U.S. movie studio turned down the opportunity to distribute the film.

Chow was convinced that the Turtles would be a hit, so much so that he spent $10 million to have a team headed by Jim Henson design and make the lifelike figures to which the Turtles' success owes so much. The film, with human beings inside Henson's figures was filmed in North Carolina. Raymond Chow's instincts were right, and the Turtles have become this Hong Kong-based company's biggest United States success.

What the Reviewers are Saying

"There was the search for the Northwest Passage, the idea of making Trenton, N.J. the U.S. capital, the Edsel, George McGovern running for President. Now there is this idea, turning the wry, happy-spirited animated TV series about four mutated turtles into a live action movie.

"It was probably a hopeless project from the start, since the continual violence that is innocuous, cartoonish brouhaha in animation becomes troubling mayhem when inflicted on real actors in a live movie. Parents should consider carefully before exposing young children to this kind of pounding.

"The tone of the dialogue is inferior too. The disarming banter that raises the animated series above its competition is largely missing from this version of the turtles' story. Here the turtles go around saying 'D———!' Characters sneer lines such as 'You want a fist in the mouth?' The hand-to-hand combat is relentless, and a lot of the film is shot almost in the dark, as if someone pulled a plug on Jim Henson's animatronics, which were used to make the guys in turtle outfits seem more lifelike."[15]

The final opinion of People Weekly magazine's Ralph Novak: "It is grim and no fun."[16]

The Wall Street Journal's Julie Salamon "liked the movie's deliberately artificial netherworld and found it to be less frightening than many other popular children's movies ('Honey, I Shrunk The Kids' for example). But for the most part I found the Mutant Ninja Turtle experience a little like watching a film shot in a language I don't speak: I got the drift but sensed I was missing something, maybe everything." Therefore she interviewed a series of children to discover the appeal of this film and its grittiness and fighting. A seven year-old named Kirlene thought the fight scenes were exciting and didn't want to miss even a minute because, "I wanted the turtles to win." She did find the movie to be a little tense, "I was scared when Splinter was in jail. I was scared he was going to die and he is one of my favorite characters." Ten year-old Laura noted the effect of the Turtles on her little brother: "Andrew's (age four) gotten much more violent since he's into the turtles. He has swords and is always jumping on chairs going, 'Yah! Yah! Yah!' "[17]

DONATELLO

5

Getting Rich On Kids

Millions of dollars are being spent to sell the Teenage Mutant Ninja Turtles to children. And children, in turn, are spending billions of dollars each year on the Teenage Mutant Ninja Turtles' movies and related paraphernalia. In 1990, over 133 million dollars were spent at box offices, making the Turtles' movie the number four hit of the year. Ever anxious to take advantage of a trend, movie makers quickly produced a sequel. "Teenage Mutant Ninja Turtles II: The Secret of The Ooze" opened to packed theatres in early 1991. The further adventures of the sewer-dwelling, pizza-eating crime fighters grossed over 33 million dollars in the first two weeks alone. The popularity of the television show, then of the movies, has prompted the production of Turtle-related products to more than double the figure of 600 mentioned in Chapter 1. There is more Turtle paraphernalia than one could imagine. There are innumerable toys with action figures coming out at a rate of three per month. SBK Records, a new company, has produced close to one million copies of the "Teenage Mutant Ninja Turtles" rap-music sound track. Ralston Purina has been cranking out boxes of marshmallow-laden Turtle cereal. The Turtles are promoting food brands from Light & Lively yogurt to Thomas's English Muffins. There are Turtle pajamas, Turtle toothbrushes, Turtle underwear, Turtle skateboards, Turtle place mats, Turtle sheets, Turtle shampoo, Turtle key chains, Turtle lunch boxes, Teenage Mutant Ninja Turtle vanilla-flavored pizza candy, Turtle pasta dinners, Turtle pizza, Turtle peanut-butter graham cookies, even Teenage Mutant Ninja Turtle pork rinds. Movie product distributors are sending out $100,000 worth of Turtle T-shirts, baseball caps, pajamas and posters each day. There are Turtle cartoons, Turtle videos, Turtle comic books, Turtle water bottles—just about everything that a child could possibly want from the time he gets up in the morning until he goes to bed at night.

The movie and toy industries have become very sophisticated. Analysts and market researchers spend thousands of hours trying to determine what will attract a child. Toy, food and clothing companies are then given permission, "licensed," to create products with the popular name or logo. This is a promotional device used to create consumer interest in a product. The idea behind licensing is that people are more likely to buy a product that increases a line of items not produced by the same manufacturer and is a favorite ploy of movie makers in general as well as the cartoon industry. Because of the recognizability of the characters, toymakers and other manufacturers can depend on heavy sales of just about any product. The public is already familiar with the character, so they are guaranteed a market. The goal is to have a line of products readily available at the same time a movie appears in theatres or a new cartoon premiers. One product automatically provides a buyer for the other.[18] The movies or television shows essentially

36

become commercials for these products. They introduce the products and show children how to play with them. A multitude of industries bombard our children with related items in a concentrated effort to amass the almighty dollar. Not only did Turtles II encourage every child to discard their old Teenage Mutant Ninja Turtles lunch boxes, book bags and T-shirts, but this movie introduced two new companions for Shredder—Wolf and Snapping Turtle. No child's collection of action figures is complete without this addition. Especially when the target is children, licensing encourages buying a product simply because it has a certain picture on it. A product, I might add, whose price is generally much higher than a similar item without the special logo.

Cross-selling is another high-pressure marketing strategy aimed at our children. Pepsi-Cola has made frequent use of product placement in Turtles' films as has Pizza Hut. Burger King promoted the Turtles' movie before it was released and sold videocassettes. Such sophisticated techniques are beyond a child's ability to understand what is true. After seeing the Turtles drink Pepsi, any child is going to refuse that glass of milk at dinner. And, why should he be expected to eat a balanced meal of roast beef, potatoes and green beans when his heroes live on pizza? In their quest for enormous profits, manufacturers have never shown less concern for the effects their products are having on the well-being of children.

In a private survey of elementary school teachers conducted by this author, the consensus of opinion is that the Teenage Mutant Ninja Turtles do not belong in the classroom. Not only have the punching and pseudo-karate chops caused several injuries, but the general attitude of the Turtles has invaded the playground—that it is fun to hurt others. The Turtles consider it great sport to do battle. "Let's do some serious damage," is their battle cry. They continuously joke, cheer each other on, make

37

wisecracks, and seem to be having a wonderful time. For them, fighting is fun—as they and many of their advertisements say, they are a "lean green, fighting machine."

One teacher was openly distressed. She had forbidden her students to bring Turtles action figures or weapons into the classroom. This teacher used a class bookclub as a reading tool. Each month she would distribute a sheet of club book selections for her students to purchase. These books are reasonably priced and are written at the age and interest level of the students. In addition, for every twenty books purchased by the students, one additional book was sent to be included in the classroom library. With educational budgets always being tight, the bookclub is a great way for a teacher to obtain classroom materials at no cost to the school district. When she opened her bookclub packet this particular month, bold bright letters across the top of the club flyer announced that if a student purchased any three books from the sheet, he would receive a free Teenage Mutant Ninja Turtles poster. A large sample poster was included to be hung in the classroom for the students to see.

Two things were wrong here—in distributing the flyer, the teacher felt she would be sending mixed messages to her students. On one hand, the Turtles were not allowed in her classroom, but it was okay for her to advocate giving them a poster for their home. In addition, the glossy colorful poster for the classroom measured about 2 ft. wide by 3 ft. high while the free poster was 8 in. wide by 11 in. high. Children don't read the fine print, and believe anything presented to them by an adult is fact. That is why they are so vulnerable as a market to crafty advertisers. Also, many parents rely too heavily on teachers. They feel that if Mrs. Smith sent this home with little Tommy, it must be okay. Instead of investigating the situation, they believe that anything coming out of the classroom is "educational." Parent, wake up and take note of what is going on around you!

6

Turtle "Rock!"

Rock music is now being concocted for the youngest consumers with simple lyrics, gaudy costumes and lots of marketability. Called "Tot-Rock" by the New York Times, rock music's latest breakthrough is the power to draw pre-teens, grade-schoolers and pre-schoolers with their parents in tow to music stores, MTV, and rock concerts. Some of this music has been custom-made for children with simple lyrics attached to gaudy costumes and maniac performances, while the rest is a spillover from music presumably created for older listeners. For the youngest audiences, some rock stars are as much fun as real-life cartoon characters, as stimulating as Nintendo and symbolically accessible through all the artifacts clever merchandisers can devise. With MTV leading the effort, television as in previous pop eras, can target young consumers directly, and a little pre-teen appeal can mean big money.

The Teenage Mutant Ninja Turtles have taken full advantage of this phenomenon. The costumed rock band playing music said to have been written by the Turtles themselves is performing across the country in typical rock style—amid the lights and smoke of a standard hard-rock show. Their album, "Coming Out Of Their Shells," retells the Turtles' story punctuated by synthesizer-bottomed funk. The messages are uniformly positive: "You gotta fight for what is right," and "Your heart is where all the music comes from."

Like their movie analogs, rock's Ninja Turtles are easy for children to identify with. They are superheroes fond of electronic toys and fueled by pizza. The pizza theme carries over into smart merchandising as the album was introduced and initially offered for sale at Pizza Hut. This marks the second combined venture, as Pizza Hut sponsored and was featured in the "Teenage Mutant Ninja Turtles" movie. Pizza Hut is betting a small fortune on the success of this venture— $20 million for the September 1990 tour launch at Radio City Music Hall in New York. They are also sponsoring a year-long U.S. tour for the band with an international leg scheduled to follow. David Novak, the chain's senior vice-president of marketing, says that Pizza Hut will reap tremendous benefits from the live rock musicians because as anyone with kids knows, pizza is the Turtles' favorite food. Not only are they sponsoring the tour, Pizza Hut is using the singing Turtles in commercials and creating promotions around the Turtles' movie video release and sequel.

While the Ninja Turtles band is a direct spin-off of the movie and television series, it has proven successful and popular with pre-teens. There have always been songs for children, from age-old lullabies to Chipmunks records. Until recently those records were made and sold outside of the mainstream pop/rock music business, usually on independent labels. The common style was friendly, folky—a nice man with a guitar like Burl Ives entertaining youngsters.

Every few years a Saturday-morning cartoon series has featured a rock band. These bands were often based on real groups such as the Beatles, the Monkeys and the Jackson 5. Some cartoons featured fictitious bands like Josie and the Pussycats. Rock music has also shown up in children's programs like "The Muppet Show" and "Fraggle Rock." These cartoon bands were generally parodies and not considered to be commercial products. However, since the mid-1980s, music made for pre-teens and youngsters has taken a drastic turn. It now features the eletronic rythms, heavy drumbeat, and special effects of contemporary rock music. The new mode is superhuman in its dizzying dance routines and no longer homey. In recent years these youngsters have been turning up at nominally adult concerts instead of staying home with a baby-sitter. They are dancing at Michael Jackson extravaganzas, cheering for Milli Vanilli and dressing like Madonna.

What has brought about this significant change? In the 1980's rock video became a television staple, supplied 24-hours per day on MTV. Rock was no longer a sonic abstraction on the radio or out of reach on older brother and sister's delicate LP's. It was now available on every cable network, in videos that were kin to both commercials and cartoons, using the visual language of television that every American child has been weaned on. MTV's early hitmakers including Culture Club, Madonna, Cindi Lauper and Michael Jackson wore bright, outlandish outfits and danced like the cartoon characters come to life. As children's programming, they offered more fun than cheaply animated cartoons not to mention better music and a contagious sense of excitement. Too many parents thought it cute when their children began to imitate Cindi Lauper's skipping or Michael Jackson's moonwalk.

41

Parents in their naivetee encouraged these children to mimic the stars and permitted them to watch the music videos unrestrained. Lip-syncing contests are held in elementary schools across the United States. This interest in rock music has in turn created a market consisting of ever younger children. As always in popular culture, television and films have bent to the demand and included even more tot-rock. It can be heard in almost every Saturday morning and after-school children's program. The purpose of this rock music isn't to debase children, but to channel their consumption. "In its purest form tot-rock exists primarily to siphon disposable income from parents' pockets. Groups like the Ninja Turtles are simply riding a successful hype, moving into one more entertainment market niche because it's there," says music expert Jon Pareles.[19]

The Ninja Turtles band is simply another commercial enterprise which reduces its music to an accessory of multi-media tie-ins, commercials and merchandising deals. And, our children are learning from the rock music that they watch. This is visible in the way they behave towards each other and toward adults. It is visible in the way they dress and talk. Rock music unlike some other forms of entertainment encouages its fans to participate—and that is exactly what they are doing no matter what their age.

7

The Philosophy Of The Turtles

Besides Rock Music, the Teenage Mutant Ninja Turtles are said to be into the Ninja Arts. They are "skilled in the art of the Ninja."

Within the past few years American adults and children alike, from all walks of life, have come to know the "martial arts" and the "secrets of the Ninja." It is not unusual to see a man or boy dressed in the now familiar white garb of certain of the marshall arts (the Karate dresses in white, Ninja in black). One mother told me that she enrolled her son into a Karate program in order to make him more forthright (and for the exercise). It seems to have done no harm to this young man, but how do the martial arts affect others?

What is a Ninja?

The origins of the Ninja (Ninjitsu) are shrouded in mystery. The word Ninjitsu itself originated in sixth century Japan during a war between Prince Shotoku and Morija over the land of Omni. A warrior named Otomo-no-Saajin aided the victory of Prince Shotoku by secretly searching out valuable information about the enemy forces. His reward for this service was the title of Shinobi, which means "stealer-in." From this idea came the Ninjitsu.

In the beginning, a Ninja (man, or woman—she is called a kunoichi) was to gather information about the enemy and then to sabotage his operations. There were diverse kinds of spies: *indigenous,* which means natives who gather intelligence; *inside,* a spy within the enemy camp; *sleeper,* a recruit awaiting the order to proceed; *doubled,* a former spy of the enemy who had worked for both sides; and *expendable,* spies who are sent out for just one mission. All carried out missions of **espionage, assassination,** and **sabotage**.

To be a Ninja, one has to be a *hunter.* He knows the ways of his prey. He has studied their habits, their patterns of movement, and their method of movement. This knowledge helps him to attack when the enemy is most vulnerable.

A Ninja is said to be a warrior, an invisible assassin, and a wizard. To be a wizard is to be able to "stop the world" and see with the "eyes of God."

The Ninja uniform includes: (a) black ski mask, as camouflage paint or "blacking" the face is time consuming and not easily removed; (b) black over-jacket; (c) black belt or sash; (d) black coveralls, with blousing ties at the wrists and ankles; and (e) black tabi, split-toed socks made for wearing with sandals—the soft sole of the sandals not only protects the feet but also helps to muffle walking sounds.

Meditation

All of the Far Eastern martial arts place an emphasis on *meditation* in order to discipline the mind and the body. This is especially important to the Ninjitsu. They believe they have developed exercises to make keen their perception and psychological insight. This process is said to help rejuvenate the body, calm the mind, and develop inner strength.

The secret of meditation is said to be regular practice which includes perseverance, diligence, and quiet determination. Two periods per day are recommended, one soon after rising and one before going to bed. The exercise is to be performed in a quiet, darkened, well-ventilated room, neither too warm nor too cold. One is instructed to wear comfortable clothing. **Breath control is believed to be the way to proper meditation, which is called the art of consciously altering the state of mind.**

A Deadly Art?

Eliminate a sentry in order to penetrate the enemy camp, writes one author of a book of Ninja. "Move in the shadows," to "become invisible." How to attack and kill the enemy is given in gruesome detail in the books of *Ninja*. (I was shocked to find a book of Ninja containing these gruesome details in the children's section at our public library.) Some of the terms used by a "Ninjitsu assassin"—all which bring almost immediate death, are the **kidney thrust**—*driving a dagger into someone's kidney*; the **subclavian artery thrust**—*thrusting a dagger down behind the collarbone*; the **jugular thrust**—*to sever the "carotid sheath" which contains the carotid artery, jugular vein, and vagus nerve*; **slitting the throat**—*by drawing the blade of the knife across the throat at the level of the carotid cartilage*, and finally the **heart thrust**—*thrusting a knife into an artery of the heart*.

45

Target areas of the attacking Ninjitsu warrior are: the *top of head, temple, cheek, throat, forearm, armpit, solar plexus, groin, kneecap,* and *instep.*

This attacking Ninjitsu warrior is depicted in the Teenage Mutant Ninja Turtles movie, comics, etc.

The Mission

The *missions* of the Ninjitsu, according to Ashida Kim, author of Secrets Of The Ninja, are divided into three major categories:

Sabotage—includes disrupting the enemy camp as well as eliminating strategic points along the enemy perimeter which will allow an assault to succeed.

Espionage—deals with the gathering of intelligence about the enemy. This may be done surreptitiously, or data gathered by the enemy may be boldly stolen.

Assassination—is an art unto itself. It may take the form of poisons, booby traps, or murder. Needless to say, the ability to get in and out without being discovered is a prerequisite.

What is Wrong with Teenage Mutant Ninja Turtles?

Although turtles themselves are not to be feared (but not many people, especially children, would wish to encounter giant-sized turtles), I believe that Teenage Mutant Ninja Turtles are teaching social, moral and spiritual values that are not in the best interest of a child.

I wonder what was going through the minds of the creators of these giant-sized turtles when they brought things like radioactive goo, mutating chemicals, living in a sewer, a rat as a "master" or god-like figure to the turtles, and ninja violence into the picture?

While the names of the turtles remind one of artists from the Renaissance, their behavior does not. The turtles and some of the other characters are described as:

Michaelangelo is a master of the flying kick and the karate punch. His favorite weapon is the *nunchaku*.

Raphael is a prankster, whose wry humor sees the team through perilous situations while his twin daggers send enemies fleeing in panic. His favorite weapon is the *sai*.

Donatello uses his swishing quarterstaff to lay out his foes like a bowling pin. His favorite weapon is the *bo*.

Leonardo is a sword-swinging team leader. His favorite weapon is the *katana*.

Splinter is a giant rat who is the "master" of the turtles. His favorite weapon is the *nunchaku*.

Shredder (also known as Oroku Saki) an armor wearing Ninja warrior, is a master of the skill of ninjitsu. His favorite weapon is the *bo*.

Sabotage, Espionage, Assassination

The Teenage Mutant Ninja Turtles are skilled in the weapons of the Ninja which include sabotage, espionage, and assassination. Not only are the Turtles skilled in deadly weapons but in the series there are stereotypes such as Asian eyes, a giant-sized rat who is a god-like figure, the giant-sized turtles themselves, and an over-endowed female.

Questionable or adverse influences are as follows:

Savior—Splinter (god-like figure, mentor, religious leader) is the giant-sized rat that is said to have rescued the Turtles from radiation and educated them into the *Ninja Arts*. This giant rat also acts as a father to the Turtles in the cartoons, comic books, etc. Should a giant-sized rat become like God? Isn't this blasphemy?

47

Crime—The Shredder, is said to be *ruthless* and *vengeful* and has a brilliant *criminal* mind. Should we teach our children that crime pays?

Eastern Religions—Krang is the spiritual leader of Shredder. Krang speaks from his middle (stomach) where a *demonic-like* figure is visible.

Sex—In the Archie Comics April O'Neil is seen as a voluptuous and sexy female. In the movie O'Neil's skirts are so short (or she is wearing shorts that they reveal her legs almost to the top of the thigh). Should our children see women only as sex images?

Darkness—The movie (which is *rated PG* and recommended for 4 to 12 year-olds) takes place in darkness where "night action" occurs. Children are prone to be afraid of the dark. Many evil deeds are done in darkness. The Bible says . . . *men loved darkness rather than light because their deeds were evil* (John 3:19).

Weapons—Names of Ninja (lethal) weapons, their description and use are incorporated into the Teenage Mutant Ninja Turtles series.

Meditation—The Ninja uses *meditation* to obtain physical power and "inner strength." Meditation is a religion that does not accept Jesus Christ, The Messiah as the one true God.

The information I have given you in this chapter is to help you learn about the Teenage Mutant Ninja Turtles, what is behind the Ninja Arts and how they are incorporated into the Turtles. I have tried to show you how the influence of this series (whether it be toys, cartoons, comic books, videos, movies, etc.) can have an adverse affect on your child emotionally, socially, morally, and spiritually. I urge you to take a good hard look at what is behind the *philosophy* of the Teenage Mutant Ninja Turtles.

sai

katana

bo

bisento

nunchaku

LEONARDO

8

Ask A Parent, Teacher, Or Dr. Joyce Brothers

According to a November 1990 survey done by U.S. News & World Report, at the top of the most despised cartoon character list rests the Teenage Mutant Ninja Turtles.[20] People Weekly named the Turtles movie in their Worst of the Screen 1990 reviews article as well as condemning Touchstone Pictures ads for the movie "Pretty Woman" which featured the Ninja Turtles leering out from under sewer covers at Julia Roberts, saying such things as "She can sit on my shell anytime."[21]

Artistically, the original 1984 Turtle comic series was not without its pleasures, but the Archie comic and the weekday TV program are frequently negligible in craft and woefully inferior. Aesthetic questions aside, is there anything about the Turtles that is likely to be hurtful to children? The overwhelming majority of parents and colleagues questioned could not find anything definitely traumatic about the content of the comic books or television show. One noted, however ironically that radioactivity is construed as the Turtles' source of strength rather than an environmental problem. Some voiced concern over the empty, formulaic nature of the narratives. Far more expressed worry about the shameless use of the characters toward hyping their own paraphernalia, and just about everything else in the galaxy. Shallow scripts and ceaseless hucksterism have pervaded children's television almost from its inception, but programming with little else in mind than merciless merchandising has increased tremendously in recent years and has attained epic proportions with the Turtles.

The paranoid, retaliatory world view of comic and TV Turtle territory cannot be overlooked, even though there isn't much blatant gore in evidence. The virtual absence of women in this Peter Pan-like milieu is striking as well. April, the Wendy-like reporter, does link the boys to doings above, but more often than not, her investigations get them into the very trouble that provokes their belligerent natures.

Dr. Joyce Brothers points a finger at Ninja Turtle talk: "They use passwords, like 'cowabunga,' that kids can say to other kids and no one else can understand." A West Virginia mother of an eight year-old can attest to this, "He's always holding his fist in the air, shouting 'awesome' and 'excellent.' She sees it as innocent fun, but other parents do not.

"I discourage my daughter from saying 'cowabunga, dude,' and 'awesome,' " says four year-old Stephanie Edwartoski's mother, a Virginia government worker. "I hate 'awesome.' I don't want a little Valley Girl."[22]

"Actually," says Dr. Brothers, "bugging the parents is the key to the Mutant Ninjas' appeal: In order for something to become a big fad, it has to make mothers and fathers feel a little disgusted, a little uncomfortable."[23]

Critics point to the aggression in the Turtles' film as a serious concern. The Ninjas and their enemies spend the majority of their screen time fighting. Another component of this entertainment is the inevitable triumph of good over evil. The "good guys" win, under the guidance of their father figure, Splinter. At the conclusion, the lost boys who follow the evil Shredder recognize their evil ways and the community is made whole again. This implies the possibility for universal brotherhood and utopia.

In a society like ours, which strains for community in the face of diversity and individualism, the Turtles' preadolescent culture is pictured where the individual bends to the moral rules of the larger order. The "lost" boys are fiercely loyal to Shredder until he is defeated by the Turtles, then they immediately become staid Turtle followers. The thought of looking to the higher power and laws of God never enter the picture, and the viewer is left with the feeling that should a giant hamster with a black-belt defeat the four turtles, he would in turn be revered.

In the movie and cartoons, almost all of the characters are male. A world is depicted wherein girls and women can be disruptive. April O'Neil, the reporter befriended by the Turtles, is constantly in need of being rescued. Her plights repeatedly put the heroes in dangerous situations. The evil Shredder in one of the cartoons sprinkled one of the Turtles' pizzas with a love potion. As he had planned, the resulting jealousy and infighting occupied the avengers, and he was able to wreak havoc in the community at will. This attitude toward one half of the earth's population doesn't reflect a world in which women are emerging as strong leaders to be respected. The condescending attitude of these programs are implanting a prelude to adult sexism.

Junk Culture

Kenan, the four year-old son of a professor and a museum curator, claims that he "needs" Teenage Mutant Ninja Turtle paraphernalia. It is easy enough—and usually accurate—to blame his situation on cynical television producers and marketers of profitable spin-off products. But his case is, in reality, more depressing than the familiar tales of zombie-like children hypnotized by junk TV and junk toys. His mother says that he has never seen the television programs or the movie whose dialogue, mannerisms and advertising jingles now come bubbling out of him. He has learned them by toddler word-of-mouth; he is the product of junk culture.

Kenan's parents have taken pains to protect him from television's influence. They restrict his TV viewing to Sesame Street and certain select video tapes. The family reads together and they play with his carefully selected toys. What happened? Kenan has fallen under the tutelage of his friends whose parents do not closely monitor their television viewing. Their busy parents are tempted to use the TV as a babysitter. The statistics are staggering. A recent report by the National Endowment for the Humanities found that children ages two to eleven watch about 24 hours per week. By the time a young person graduates from high school, he or she will have spent almost 20,000 hours watching television—compared to 12,500 hours in the classroom.

The results of such video devotion on everything from education test scores to literacy to violence is the subject of familiar condemnation. Also familiar is the prescriptive advice to parents to protect children from the more nefarious programming. Now well-meaning parents are further assaulted by the pervasive culture generated by these shows and their products.[24]

According to a continuing 22 year study of television violence by George Gerbner, a communications professor at the University of Pennsylvania, television programs for children—mostly cartoons—have become saturated with violence. Kids' programs contain nearly five times the violence of adult prime-time programming and is extremely prevalent in "mostly humorous" violence. He said, "Violence essentially demonstrates who can dominate or terrorize whom, and humor is a sugar coating." During children's hours, 90 percent of the programs are violent.[25]

According to the Nielson Index, the average American child has watched 18,000 television murders before he or she graduates from high school. The report says, "Television did not invent violence. It just put it on the assembly line and into every home. For most viewers, the heavy doses of TV violence cultivate a sense of relative danger, mistrust, dependence . . . alienation and gloom." The more hours of TV watched, the more prevalent these feelings were.[26]

Into The Day Care Centers

Turtlemania was causing unwelcome changes at playtime, several day care teachers in Buffalo, New York said. Therefore, Teenage Mutant Ninja Turtles are no longer welcome. "The four year-old group was hit the strongest with Ninja fever," said Mary Ann Haney, director of East Aurora Community Nursery. She has told parents to keep their offsprings' Turtle toys at home. **"It manifests itself with lots of physical aggressive activities, karate chops, flying feet and that sort of thing.** The play really changed when the children got the Turtles out of their cubbies. Everything would focus on them. Even though we have rules about weapons here, the blocks would be turned into guns. It was harder and harder to control."

"They all started calling each other Butt Head and Party Dude and making all their Legos into swords and weapons," added teacher Ginnie Monthony.[27]

SPLINTER

9

Brainwashing Our Kids

Have you actually sat down with your children to watch
Teenage Mutant Ninja Turtles? In one half-hour episode of
the series, I counted no less than 15 commercials. To a
background of rap or rock music, savy children in brightly-
colored trendy clothes and hair styles were shown having
fun—and selling everything from breakfast cereals and
burgers to Ninja Turtles toys. Instructions were given as to
exactly how to play with these toys in keeping with the
storyline.

Ninja Influence Outside of the United States

Millions of children overseas are just discovering the
reptilian charms of Teenage Mutant Ninja Turtles. In Mexico
they are called Karate Turtle Warriors. The superheroes are
already big in Brazil, Malaysia, and Britain. When the cartoon
characters made an appearance at Singapore airport, 30,000

children showed up yelling, "Yo, dude!" The cartoons premiered in Spring of 1990 in New Zealand and much of Europe including Italy, Germany and Holland. Another potential is the soon-to-be-exploited market in Japan, birthplace of both the Ninja-warrior tradition and the radioactive creature movie genre.

Early in 1990 the Turtles invaded England. However, when the children's BBC began running the popular cartoon series, it insisted that it should be retitled "Hero Turtles" rather than "Ninja Turtles" to discourage children from taking up martial arts. Britain isn't the only country that is steeling itself against the invasion of the Turtles.

Blaming the Teenage Mutant Ninja Turtle craze for an increase in playground aggression, many schools throughout the country of Australia have banned the Turtle toys from classrooms and have warned students to leave their Ninja swords, nunchakus and sais at home.

The widespread concern about the Turtles' effect on children through both the television series and the movie prompted David Ross, a primary school principal in the suburb of Hartwell to challenge the series. "Some of our younger children were being hurt unintentionally as they were 'chopped' by their playmates using imaginary swords," the teacher of five to twelve year-olds said in a New York Times interview. "What basically Ninja Turtles comes down to is solving problems by force which is incompatible with our aim for a friendly, cooperative and caring school."

Mr. Ross' action in alerting parents about possible harmful side effects of the show drew support throughout the country.

"I realized then we had stumbled upon something which was of serious concern to many people," he said. "Most teachers are opposed to those shows which depict violence as we have to field the consequent behavior problems at school."[28]

The Australian Children's Television Action Committee, a community-financed organization that is represented on the official Australian Broadcasting Tribunal, asserts that there is a direct link between Ninja Turtles and increased aggression by young children.

"The series is aimed at six year-olds, and at that age children cannot distinguish between fantasy and reality," reports Mary Murdoch, spokeswoman for the committee. "It is our view they are learning that violence, as used by good guys, is the answer to all problems and this is then translated into their behavior."[29]

The Australian Council for Children's Films and Television says that the series also breaches advertising standards set by the Australian Broadcasting Tribunal, the national television regulatory group.

"The show is designed to sell Ninja Turtle products and not provide quality entertainment," said Barbara Biggins, a television officer for the council. "Because it is financially beneficial to the networks, that genre of program threatens to squeeze out genuine programming for younger viewers."[30]

Despite the widespread concern about the Turtles' effect on children, both the Ninja Turtle movie and television series are scoring record ratings. More than 200,000 Australian children see the movie each weekend, and the animated television series has a 73 percent share of the audience in its 4 PM time slot. Prohibiting children from taking Ninja fighting toys to school is one step in the right direction, but it will take far more action on the part of educators, parents and television officials to eliminate the anti-social behavior prompted by the Teenage Mutant Ninja Turtles and other violent television programs and movies.

SHREDDER

10

Turtles In The Toy Box

Toy designers and their corresponding cartoon writers will not change as long as they continue to be rewarded for the things they do. Parents need to take a good look at the toys that are in their child's toy box, to decide what is good for the child.

Toys and games promoting violence and occult practices are growing in popularity. War toys comprise the leading category of toy sales in the United States, with G.I. Joe being challenged for first place by Teenage Mutant Ninja Turtles. It is closely followed in popularity by several other cartoon-based toys: Real Ghostbusters, Robocop, Dick Tracy, and Batman. The continued popularity of He-Man and She-Ra has kept those toys on the shelves and the cartoons on the air several times each day. The occult imagery of the Smurfs, Scooby Doo, and the Care Bears fill several slots in the television schedule daily. In addition to violent cartoons, our children are being bombarded with advertisements promoting violent toys.

Although the real world is filled with violence and murders, Satanism, and the occult, those who are Christians should not expose their children to unGodly acts. Children must live in the world and be exposed to violence at some time in their life. However, a parent should not invite violence and the occult into the home to be a part of their children's play time. Their children should not be associated with toys and games that feature occult philosophies and phenomena because they glorify Satan and his battle against the church. Matthew 6:24 states:

> No man can serve two masters: for either he will hate the one and love the other; or else he will hold to one and despise the other. Ye cannot serve God and mammon.

Toy stores can barely keep their shelves filled with the violent, broad assortment of Teenage Mutant Ninja Turtles toys. Most of these toys have been introduced on the cartoon, causing immediate demand for each item by a ready market.

The weekly series is full of bitter satire and violence. Some of the toys symbolize this:

Teenage Mutant Ninja Turtles Toys
(Playmates *Wacky Action* figures)

Sewer-Swimmin' Donatello   a wind-up sewer-spyin' reptile with swimmin' action!

Sword-Slicin' Leonardo   a wind-up radical reptile with slash'n thrash action!

Rock N Roll Michaelangelo   a wind-up party reptile with twist-wrist Ninja action!

Breakfightin' Raphael   a wind-up streetwise reptile with streetwise breakfightin' action!

Creepy Crawlin' Splinter   a wind-up rat with sewer slithering action!

Slice & Dice Shredder   a wind-up madman with spinin' slice'n dice blades!

Wacky Walkin' Mouser   a wind-up robotic rat trap with an appetite for turtles. Motorized walkin' and chompin' action!

Other Teenage Mutant Ninja Turtles Toys

Retrocatapult (a cannon)   shoots green ooze

Footski   a brain-sucking sewer machine

Sewer Seltzer Cannon   squirts water

Flushomatic High-Tech   the ultimate torture device
Toilet Trap

Needlenose (Meg. Militant)   a blood-sucking military mutant
                                    mosquito

More Turtles Toys

Oozey	**Footcruiser**
Pizza Thrower	**Cheapskate**
Retromutagen ooze	**Knucklehead**
Sludgemobile	**Sewer Force Sword**
Mutant Maker	**Sewer Explorer Belt**
Mutant Killer Bee	**Sewer Sky Goggles**
Mutant Module	**Sewer Tubes**
Plunger Gun	**Sewer Artillery**
Turtle Trooper	**Sewer Play Set**
Turtle Blimp	**Sewer Party Wagon**
Turtle Copter	**Sewer Psycho Cycle**
Turtle Battle	**Sewer Dragster**
Crazy Artillery	**Scumbug and his Turtle Exterminating Gun**

Note: This (not to mention a line of Plush toys), is not
a complete list of every Teenage Mutant Ninja Turtles
toy that is available—there are more!

Violent toys enable children to rehearse violent behavior which is seen on television or in the movies. This increases the likelihood that they will incorporate these violent scenes into their world of "let's pretend" and later into their lives. The Teenage Mutant Ninja Turtles teach that every problem can be handled with a gun, sword, or sai, nunchakus, bo or katana. They portray war and fighting as fun and give the impression that good guys never get fatally injured or lose a battle. These scenes desensitize children to pain and violence by showing thousands of violent acts. Fighting is glorified. Fighting is fun. What type of adult will a child become, who lives on a diet of violence?

11

What You Can Do About It!

What you do is important. You are not only accountable for your own actions, you are also accountable for the effects those actions have on others.

Television portrays the concept that fighting is glamorous—it is chosen by the hero as the first solution to a problem. It is our responsibility to point out this fallacy to our children.

We must examine what we want for our children. We exert one of the biggest influences on our child's choice of entertainment. A child must learn to make judgements based on quality, and we must teach them to do this. Therefore, parents must have good judgement themselves concerning the amount and quality of the television programming that we watch. What type of an example are we setting? In spite of our differences, most people living in a free society would agree that we want to live civilly, safely and peaceably. Consider that Teenage Mutant Ninja Turtles and other violent programs encourage behaviors that threaten a civilized society.

Continued unnecessary violence is addictive. It can be entertainment of a high order, and young people can get hooked on it. When boys and girls are bombarded by the violence spewed from television and films, they can lose interest in dramatizations that pose problems resolved through thoughtful, sometimes laborious efforts of a peaceful nature. It is easier to identify with the action figure than the thinker. Violent action can be the result of thought insufficient to develop other solutions. It can be a dangerous form of escapism to children fenced in by regulations in every aspect of their lives. Children like to see "fairness," good or right triumph over "unfairness," evil or wrong, but the depiction of violence can confuse them. It can persuade children that violence is the only appropriate or possible solution—whereas if a more thorough analysis of the situation were made, any number of peaceful alternatives may be found.

Turn Off That Trash!

Turn off that trash that spews from your television set and create a peaceful environment for your children. If you want your children to adopt cooperative behaviors, make certain that you handle tough situations without becoming aggressive yourself. Set a good example for your children. At the same time, don't expose them to violent role models. If children want to watch a character on television who is violent, interest them in another program or turn off the TV and find another activity for them.

Studies point out that the thousands of hours youngsters spend in front of the televison during their formative and creative years actually reduce active play. Television does nothing to induce your child to discover, to learn on his own. When watching the television, the child becomes "hypnotized." He stops all movement. True play is active and interactive, with people or things. Except for a very few, most programs (even "educational" ones) stop play, and the imagination.

Teachers today have noticed that children do not play as they once did. A certain passivity has set in. Dramatic play is not so dramatic. Imagination seems to be less imaginative. Most blame television for this turn of events. Experts advise a maximum of one hour of television per day for children of all ages. It may be hard to enforce, but your child's resourcefulness, independence, and creativity may depend on it.

The World Of Let's Pretend

The influence of toys forms a child's character. This fact is undisputed. If we also consider that a child learns through his environment, we can begin to realize the powerful impact that the toy industry has on the minds of our children. Therefore, when manufacturers join with producers of television programs and movies to flood the market with items surrounding an individual character or program such as the Ninja Turtles, they are creating an artificial environment that is extremely inviting to children. The television shows the characters and instructs our children in how to play with them. The toy industry continues to bombard the child with accessories which "magically" appear on the next exciting episode. The world of "let's pretend" becomes simply an imitation of the fantasy universe pictured on television. Rather than stimulating a child's imagination, toys of this type stifle it by channeling the child's play time along the lines of the TV show he watches.

71

The Hard-Sell Technique

The toy industry works chiefly through impulse buying based on hard-sell advertising directed at the children themselves and on sophisticated packaging intended to capture parents' immediate interest.

We are too easily seduced by bright colors and exaggerated promotional claims. Parents must be wary of all of the advertising devices and watch out for children's programming that may be too persuasive and implant psychological images that lead to preoccupation with cartoon characters or their toy replicas. This is especially true with younger children who are not able to deal with the hard-sell that takes place in many programs. Bruce Watkins, Assistant Professor of the Communications Department at the University of Michigan says that children under seven years old are even more influenced by these types of shows. He said, "One element of these shows that is really unfortunate is that they were created to sell toys as opposed to entertain children."[31]

Peer Pressure

The pressure to buy toys does not come entirely from the television. Children are easily enticed by fads, and owning the "in" toy is extremely important to them. Peer pressure or wanting to belong to the "gang" is often the reason for a child to want the most popular or newest in a series of toys. He wants to "fit in" on the playground or in school. A child needs to feel that he is part of the group and will go to almost any length to prove his suitability. He believes that his popularity with other children depends entirely on his having certain toys. After all, it is much easier for a child to enter a game of Teenage Mutant Ninja Turtles if he has the latest equipment in his pocket. This idea of needing to belong and needing the newest toys is fostered on every television commercial aired. These vignettes of life picture

72

children happily playing together, of course with the sponsor's product.

Parents must prepare themselves to meet the challenge of competing with the television mentality. They must provide alternatives to the Saturday morning marathon cartoon diet that is followed by a shopping spree at the local toy store.

What You Can Do About It!

Parents should continuously monitor what their children are watching. Don't use the TV as a baby-sitter. Be there for your children. Explain TV programs to them. Tell them exactly why you disapprove of the Teenage Mutant Ninja Turtles, G.I. Joe or He-Man.

Seize the opportunity to discuss the unreality of commercials. Explain to your children how camera angles enhance the appearance of a toy, or that a close-up picture makes it look larger. It is never too early to teach your child to be an informed consumer.

"All The Other Kids Have One"

Children should strive to be individuals, and not be like Johnny or Mary next door. Television fosters the idea of being like everyone else. Children want every toy advertised because "everyone else already has it." As a result, television makes certain toys, which Christians find totally unacceptable, appear to be attractive. Many times, the ads even convince parents that the toys are harmless and cute. In the end, Satan wins. He gets a hold on the child and his imagination.

As parents, we need to recognize that when it comes to toys, there is a lot of nonsense we need to deal with. It comes directly from the toymakers, from our kids, and from ourselves. However, once we identify the problem, there are steps we can take to define what is best for our children. The obvious answer is to set limits on both TV viewing and

73

TV-related buying. The earlier you set up the pattern of being a selective viewer and consumer, the better. Preselect the programs that are to be watched, and stick to it. Never, never simply turn the TV on and leave it on for the entire day. Make a schedule and stick to it. Take the time to watch some of the cartoon shows with your child. Discuss with them the things that disturb you.

Find a better form of entertainment for your children. Remember that children's television is not the only form of entertainment that can stimulate children's imagination and play. Books, movies, videos, story cassettes, music, computers, theater, art, dance, and museums are readily available. Children need a variety of experiences to grow and become human. They need to exercise their minds as well as their muscles. Even more, they need your time, your example, and your guidance.

Giving toys should never be a substitute for yourself. If you give a child an excessive amount of toys without giving personal time, your child will know it. Children can easily become demanding and self-centered because of not getting what they really want—your undivided attention. Gifts are even more loving if you come with them. Sit and play with your child. Enjoy a board game with him. Having tea with a new set of dishes or working on a hobby, model boat or car together is often a rich and memorable moment between parent and child. It is wise to take the time to shop carefully and, when you can, take your children with you. They can see for themselves how many toys there are. They will better understand that their toy box could never hold everything. Do not overdo what you give your child in objects. Give your child what he needs, not what will impress, overpower or control him with dependency.

Make Up Your Own Mind!

The Bible warns,

> *My people are destroyed for lack of knowledge: because thou hast rejected knowledge, I will also reject thee, that thou shalt be no priest to me: seeing thou has forgotten the law of thy God, I will also forget thy children* (Hosea 4:6).

Don't let the television influence you concerning what to buy for your child. It is up to you, the parent or guardian, to thoroughly investigate the kinds of toys that are on the market today. It is up to you to say "No" when your child urges you to purchase toys that you believe are not right for him or her. Don't let your love for the child persuade you to live under the control of the advertising media. **Make up your own mind!**

Bibliography

1. Hammer, Joshua and Annetta Miller, *Ninja Turtle Power*, Newsweek, April 16, 1990, p. 60.

2. Schneider, Karen S., Maria Eftimiades, John Griffiths, Janine di Giovanni and Champ Clark, *Cowabunga! Unshelled, These Teenage Mutant Ninja Actors Kick off The 1990 Silly Season*, People Weekly, April 23, 1990, p. 50.

3. *Ninja Turtles Hot on Christmas Toy Lists*, New Era, Lancaster, Pennsylvania, December 12, 1988, p. B10.

4. Coward, Rosalind, *Invasion of the Turtles*, New Statesman & Society, August 24, 1990, p. 25.

5. Goldman, Kevin, *Ninja Turtles Juggernaut Demolishes Box Office Record*, The Wall Street Journal, April 3, 1990, p. B1.

6. Ibid.

7. Greenberg, Harvey R., *Just How Powerful Are Those Turtles?* The New York Times, April 15, 1990, p. H1.

8. Ibid.

9. Hammer, p. 61.

10. Ibid.

11. Canby, Vincent, *What Beauty And The Beast Have In Common*, The New York Times, June 3, 1990, p. H13.

12. Van Gelder, Lawrence, *At The Movies*, The New York Times, May 11, 1990, p. C10.

13. Ibid.

14. Ibid.

15. Novak, Ralph, *Picks & Pans*, People Weekly, April 2, 1990, p. 15.

16. Ibid.

17. Salamon, Julie, *Ninja Turtles, From Sewers, Lure Kids*, Wall Street Journal, April 12, 1990, p. A12.

18. Robie, Joan Hake, Turmoil In The Toy Box II, Lancaster, Pennsylvania: Starburst Publishers, 1989, pp. 32-33.

19. Pareles, Jon, *Tot-Rock: A Mini-Boom in Pop Music*, The New York Times, September 30, 1990, p. H1.

20. *Down With Turtles,* U.S. News & World Report, November 12, 1990, p. 93.

21. *What A Year,* People Weekly, December 31, 1990-January 7, 1991, p. 10.

22. Schneider, p. 50.

23. Ibid.

24. Bahrani, Yasmine, *My Nephew, the Ninja Turtle,* The Washington Post, April 15, 1990, p. D5.

25. Dart, Bob, *Wham! Bam! Cartoon Violence No Laughing Matter,* Intelligencer Journal, Lancaster, Pennsylvania, January 26, 1990, p. B7.

26. Ibid.

27. *Day care centers banning Teenage Mutant Ninja Turtles,* Sunday News, Lancaster, Pennsylvania, April 8, 1990, p. A7.

28. *Ninja Influence on Australian Youth,* The New York Times, August 16, 1990, p. C20.

29. Ibid.

30. Ibid.

31. Robie, p. 37.

Other Sources

Gubernick, Lisa, *Turtle Power,* Forbes, May 28, 1990.

Fine, Gary Alan, *Those Preadolescent Ninja Turtles,* The New York Times, June 2, 1990.

Herbeck, Bobby, *Teenage Mutant Ninja Turtles—The Storybook Based On The Movie,* New York, New York, Random House, 1990.

Kim, Ashida, *Secrets Of The Ninja,* New York, New York, The Berkley Publishing Group, 1981.

Lipman, Joanne, *Ninja Turtles May Be In Danger Of Overexposure By Marketers,* Wall Street Journal, August 1, 1990.

Picks & Pans' Worst of Screen, People Weekly, December 31, 1990-January 7, 1991.

Simpson, Janice, *Lean, Green and on the Screen,* Time, April 2, 1990.

Wallberg, Larry, *Turtles Devour Disney,* Wall Street Journal, November 14, 1990.

Books & Tapes by Starburst Publishers

The Great Pretender —Rose Hall Warnke & Joan Hake Robie
(trade paper) ISBN 0914984039 **$8.95**

Devotion in Motion —Joan Hake Robie
(trade paper) ISBN 0914984004 **$4.95**

You Can Live In Divine Health —Joyce Boisseau
(trade paper) ISBN 0914984020 **$6.95**

To My Jewish Friends With Love —Christine Hyle
(booklet) 0006028098 **$1.00**

Turmoil In The Toy Box video —Phil Phillips
(90 min. video tape—VHS only) 0006563589 **$34.95**

The Truth About Dungeons & Dragons —Joan Hake Robie
(cassette tape) ISBN 091498425X **$7.95**

Turmoil In The Toy Box II —Joan Hake Robie
(cassette tape) ISBN 0914984268 **$7.95**

Purchasing Information

Most listed books and tapes are available from your favorite Bookstore, either from current stock or special order. You may also order direct from STARBURST PUBLISHERS. When ordering enclose full payment plus $2.00* for shipping and handling ($2.50* if Canada or Overseas). Payment in US Funds only. Please allow two to three weeks for delivery within the USA. Make checks payable to and mail to STARBURST PUBLISHERS, P.O. Box 4123, LANCASTER, PA 17604. Prices subject to change without notice. Catalog available upon request.

* We reserve the right to ship your order the least expensive way. If you desire first class (domestic) or air shipment (overseas) please enclose additional funds as follows: First Class within the USA enclose $2.00. Airmail Canada and Overseas enclose 30% of total order. These amounts must be added to the base shipping costs listed in the previous paragraph. All remittance must be in US Funds.

THE THINGS
I HAD TO LEARN

Loretta Young

———

The Things
I Had to Learn

as told to

HELEN FERGUSON

THE **BOBBS-MERRILL** COMPANY, INC.
A SUBSIDIARY OF HOWARD W. SAMS & CO., INC.
Publishers • INDIANAPOLIS • NEW YORK

To . . .

OUR MOTHERS . . .
WITHOUT WHOM
I'D NOT BE HERE TO
LEARN AND TELL

NOR I TO BE TOLD TO . . .

CONTENTS

THE THINGS
I HAD TO LEARN

CLOSE-UPS *of Loretta*

(*without a camera*)

by

HELEN FERGUSON

ONE September Sunday evening in 1953, on the miniature home screens of TV, an Academy Award winning motion-picture actress swirled through a door.

She was graceful. She was beautiful. She was indisputably a star. She was also something the TV screens didn't show—a lady who'd burned her bridges behind her. The kind of fore-sighted lady, who in another century, believing and daring, packed her silver candelabra in a covered wagon and left security to seek the promise.

Presented by NBC, sponsored by Procter & Gamble, her welcome and staying power in a brand-new medium would be decided by the nation's TV-set owners—as formidable a challenge as the Rockies had been to the pioneer ladies she emulated.

A child extra at four, a juvenile bit-player at eleven, a studio contractee at twelve, a star—in adult roles—at fourteen, she grew up in, of and with Hollywood. She is its product. Its studio stages are her "home town." She reached the top and made it her permanent address, compassed by accepted advice and instructions, self-discipline, conscientious application and that indispensable, old-fashioned American success-ingredient—hard work.

Acting is her job. She respects and is bound by its obligations and responsibilities—and is as enthusiastic about its rewards and Awards as when, a pre-teenager, her dreams were taller than she was.

By this time I'm sure, but won't take it for granted, that everyone knows: Gretchen Young was born in Salt Lake City on January 6, 1913, the third child of Earl and Gladys Royal Young. One day in 1916, Earl Young left for work. He never returned. Mrs. Young, with four small ones to support, transplanted her beautiful brood to Hollywood and opened a boarding house. When brother-in-law Ernest Traxler, an assistant director at Famous Players-Lasky, suggested her little girls be allowed to try their luck as child-extras at the studio, Mrs. Young accepted the suggestion, to the delight of her older daughters, Polly Ann and Betty Jane (Sally Blane), and when Gretchen was four she too made her cinematic "debut."

By the time she was six, she had decided to be a star. In her lexicon, decision and determination have always been synonymous and at fourteen, as the tightrope walker in *Laugh, Clown, Laugh,* starring Lon Chaney, her sixty-five inches of reedy gracefulness encased in padding and symmetricals created by the wardrobe department, to provide the curves which nature had not yet provided—she did become a star.

First under contract to First National then to Warner Bros. and later to Fox and to Twentieth Century, she flitted from picture to picture after *Laugh, Clown, Laugh.* Her classroom was a corner of any studio stage on which she was working, and her tutor waited for her between scenes.

When talking-pictures abolished the subtitle era and vanquished many silent-picture-greats, the hazards of voice and sound, which terrified Hollywood's citizenry, didn't panic Loretta. Encased now in self-confidence, she assured herself that, whatever it took to survive, she had it.

Twenty years and seventy-four pictures after *Laugh, Clown, Laugh,* she stood in the Motion Picture Academy Awards' spotlight while the audience cheered the greatest "darkhorse" winner, the all-time "upset," in Oscar's Hollywood sweepstakes. Her sparkling, incredulous eyes were riveted on the golden Oscar clutched in her hand. Her smile was as bright as the spotlight. Surprised, elated—but literal, as always—

"At long last!" she said.

And the delighted crowd cheered all over again.

At the first split-second lull in all the backstage excitement —photographers, reporters, congratulations from other winners

—she ran, I "at heel," to the nearest telephone, dialed her mother's number. A sweet, I-was-sound-asleep-voice answered.

"Mamma! Mamma!! I won. I *won*. I WON!!!" she caroled.

"Why, that's lovely, Gretchen," Mamma said. "What did you win, dear?"

I remember the first time I saw Loretta Young—the first off-screen time, that is—it was nearly nine o'clock at one of Mrs. Basil Rathbone's fabulous, unforgettable parties.

A sudden converging of the roving photographers directed all eyes to the gardenia-outlined entrance of the huge tent which Ouida Rathbone had converted into a fragrant, fairyland setting.

"Loretta Young!"

The swift whisper of the assembled glamour-greats ballooned into a small thunder of excitement—the photographers massed at the entrance, held their cameras focused.

For a Dietrich, a Swanson, a Harlow, a Grable, this excitement was routine, understandable. But for the orphan-girl in *Zoo in Budapest?* The crisp cool nurse of *The White Parade?* The legendary *Ramona?* The wistful waif of *Man's Castle?* I didn't get it. But, there it was. The tribute of spontaneous attention from the people she'd grown up with.

Cesar Romero, tall, dark and handsome, came through the entry-way, shaking his head at the photographers, his hand gesturing toward his mouth; and the photogs, in a mystifying unity, lowered their cameras. Then there was a long breath of silence in the big tent as, flanked by James Stewart and David Niven, Loretta Young stepped through the gardenia "frame." It was quite an entrance!

There was an extraordinarily brilliant sparkle about her smile, as she paused and, in turn, thanked each of the boys who'd held the fire of their flash bulbs, and I remembered an item in Louella's column that morning.

To all intents and purposes Loretta Young was a glamour girl—a great, big movie star. In fact? Loretta Young was a youngster under sentence to one of the most difficult-to-bear of all teen-age trials.

Miss Loretta Young wore great, big, bright, shining gold braces across her front teeth!

By the time I actually met her, the great, big gold braces were long gone, and the legends of Loretta were many, tall and varied. (If ever anyone grew up in a brighter gold-fish bowl, it surely was way, way before my time!)

Ours was a business appointment. The in-person loveliness of Loretta Young, now and newly Mrs. Tom Lewis, was no surprise, but the firm, strong hand-clasp, straightforward questions and the competence with which she directed our interview certainly were surprises! I discovered that for all her wide-eyed youngness, her fragile-seeming femininity, this was no fortune-favored doll-face. This was an intelligent, trained and disciplined professional.

When she had all the information she wanted, she said, "I

want to think about our discussion for a day or two. I'll call you." Our business interview was ended, and suddenly she was all charming hostess. "I'd love for you to have tea with me—or a cocktail? Do you have time?" she asked.

Of course I "had time." If she thought well of our business discussion, she'd become one of my clients. It would be my job to know this girl—to know her very well indeed. All the Public Relations facets of her career would be entrusted to me.

She had thought well of our business discussion. Her call came before noon the next day. That was just a little less than two decades ago—in which time I have, indeed, come to know her very well.

Sure and clear in all I know of her is the consistency—the literal dependability of Loretta Young. Girl and woman. I know that what she says, she means; what she says she will do, she does. And, let's face it, what she wants, she gets.

How well I know that from the day Mrs. Tom Lewis became its president, the needs of St. Anne's Foundation, which supports the St. Anne's Maternity Hospital for Unmarried Mothers and sponsored the establishment of The Holy Family Adoption Service, were constantly on her mind. Often, and of necessity, too busy for a lot of things, in all her seven years as the Foundation's president, she was never too busy to do whatever could be of any possible help to St. Anne's.

During World War II, employees at the Lockheed plant paid

a dollar a month to the "Buck-of-the-Month Club," which, each month, presented a sizable check to a selected charity.

Loretta's voice was ecstatic when I told her that St. Anne's Foundation was being considered, and its president would have to address the membership at its next meeting—to establish St. Anne's deserving.

The date was set: At the Lockheed Plant, Burbank.

That it was one of sunny Southern California's unsunny, dense-fog early mornings didn't explain Loretta's uncharacteristic, stolid silence on the long drive to Lockheed, for she is a gal who really loves to "visit" any time, any place and particularly with any new acquaintance. She has to find out what said new acquaintance is interested in. And *why*. Her curiosity about people is insatiable.

But on this morning she sat very straight, very still and silent, in the corner of the limousine while the nice young man from Lockheed who was our escort and I chattered aimlessly —acutely conscious of the fact that our fellow-passenger spoke not at all and, isolated in a cocoon of silence, stared unblinkingly at the road ahead.

Obviously, something was requiring her utmost control. But I knew better than to ask any questions. Loretta is not the least bit shy about telling whatever she wants to tell. I knew that whatever this was, she'd tell me in her own good time and manner or—never tell me at all.

At Lockheed she went through her assignment, wearing a smile as bright as St. Anne's hoped-for dollars. The quiet simplicity and sincerity of her appeal for St. Anne's was deeply moving, and the Foundation was assured of its "Buck-of-the-Month Club" check.

Still wearing that smile, she sat on the platform during all the other speeches and, at the end of the program, autographed hundreds of eagerly proffered slips of paper until the work whistle blew and the crowd started to disperse.

Then she grasped my hand, very tightly, and whispered, "May we go now?" There was an urgency in her tone, but that smile didn't waver as I rushed her through the essential goodbyes, or as she waved and smiled from the car until we were outside the gate.

Abruptly then, her "appearance" ended. The smile was erased. And again, she sat still and straight—tight-lipped, remote, controlled.

Then, I *knew!*

The driver and I exchanged a look of sudden understanding in the rear-view mirror. He nodded, slanted a look at her over his shoulder, gentled his speed, turned into a side road, coasted onto the road-shoulder and braked the car. He got out and opened the rear door.

"Come now, Mrs. Lewis," he said kindly. And, with an almost tender gallantry, helped Mrs. Tom Lewis out of the car.

Loretta Young, feeling as she had upon awakening this morning, would have automatically canceled working at the studio. The president of St. Anne's hadn't even considered canceling her appointment to be of service to St. Anne's because of a revealing, early-morning discomfort.

Nor had it occurred to Mrs. Tom Lewis to share her early-morning discovery with anyone until she had reached Major Tom Lewis and shared it first with him.

I'll always remember the day, at Loretta's house, when I was reciting the details of my sole niece's forthcoming wedding. It's no secret that I'm as doting an aunt as ever cluttered a family-tree, and as I was describing her wedding gown Loretta went to her dressing table, opened her jewel-case. She held up a pearl and diamond necklace with an exquisite medallion pendant. As she looked admiringly at the sparkling, spectacular example of the jeweler's art she said:

"This is the first *real* jewelry I ever owned. I thought I'd never finish paying for it! D'you think Barbara'd like to wear it with her wedding gown? It'd be a kind of nifty 'something borrowed,' wouldn't it?"

It was a glamorous motion-picture star's adornment. It would have been much too "nifty" for our very young bride, but I loved Loretta for offering something so meaningful to her—to someone who is incomparably meaningful to me.

Loretta's hopelessly underdeveloped sense of fear was always compelling us to try to inveigle her into practicing at least a smidgin of caution. Like, for instance, locking a door?

In the middle of one Thursday night, Beatrice, Loretta's maid, telephoned me at home. She whispered that she didn't want to rouse the household, but she knew there was a prowler around the house. She'd already tip-toed through all the down-stairs rooms and found no one inside the house, but she was sure anyway.

I alerted the police and the private patrol, and first thing in the morning (Friday) after discussing the matter with Tom, had all the locks changed. New keys were distributed to all members of the Lewis household on Saturday morning.

We gave Loretta a bright new key, too. And we gave her a real caution-inspiring lecture—we hoped.

She heard us out politely, gaily assured us of her understanding, earnestly examined her bright new key while she murmured the reminder, "Everything's insured anyway.

"I think you're all crazy," she then said sweetly. "But I'll really try to remember to lock all the doors—if that'll make the two of you any happier."

That evening, like a good little girl, in painstaking, conscientious obedience, Loretta made the first door-locking tour of her whole life and gave her full, perfectionist's attention to it. Then she and Tom went to a party.

Sunday morning, Beatrice called me again and I went over there fast!

Facts upon arrival:

All the doors, but one, were locked.

A second-story job of incredible skill had been most successfully effected.

All of Loretta's jewels and all of her furs were gone.

Only the two-inch ledge outside the upstairs sitting room and a tiny slit in the window screen were "souvenirs" of the burglar's entry. The wide-open door to the garden proclaimed his point of exit.

The police came, the private patrol men came, the photographers and reporters came.

On Monday morning, Loretta called me. She said, "Well, this'll teach me—I hope! I hope I'll never again offer to *lend* something lovely to someone. I should have *given* my necklace to Barbara for a wedding present. But, no, oh no, I couldn't do that—I had to hang on to it! So now I haven't got it at all."

I couldn't think of anything to say when she paused.

"It wasn't insured," she said slowly. "The girl in the office forgot to renew over half of our insurance. The poor little thing. She's so upset!"

"I can understand that," I said flatly.

"Well, she just forgot," she defended. "Anyway, it does serve me right. I *should* have given my necklace to Barbara. That's all there is to it." The last word was hers. That's all there was to it.

Not a word, not a peep about the irony of the locked doors, the new keys, the alerted police patrols, the alerted private police patrols, the caution-lectures!

When the Beverly Hills police caught the burglar, Loretta asked me to go with her to Police Headquarters to identify whatever of hers was in the loot the police had found cached in this Raffles' apartment. No novice, he had the complete equipment of a master-jeweler in his apartment, too.

His cache was a veritable treasure chest of sparkling gems and shining, precious metal. Every priceless article he'd stolen had been broken up, the metal melted. There were unset diamonds galore; there were pearls and emeralds and rubies. There were a dozen ingots of platinum and gold.

I can still see Loretta beside the long, wide table, gazing reflectively at that display of glittering, meaningless, unidentifiable, precious stones. I can still hear what she said:

"Why, in heaven's name, didn't I give Barbara my necklace?"

Only once have I seen Loretta's self-containment fail. It was when we went to visit The Lighthouse, the New York school for blind children.

The bright-faced young woman, who fairly glowed with excitement when she greeted us, led us to the elevator. She said she'd "seen" all of Loretta's pictures and it meant so much to her and to everyone at the school to "see" her in person.

In the elevator, Loretta's eyes widened with amazement. Her lips formed the words, without sound, "She's blind!"

She was. She was also a thrilling example of triumph over handicap. Admiringly, we followed her swift, sure guidance through the halls to the huge classroom where the officials of the school were waiting. The greetings over, the children were sent for.

These little ones without sight, from two to six years old, entered the room in pairs, each child holding the hand of the teacher between each pair. Their faces wore eager, expectant smiles.

A little boy in the third pair was about two. My heart skipped a beat. He looked exactly like little Peter Lewis.

Loretta was talking with the teachers on the other side of the room. She turned, smiling, to greet the children and saw that little two-year-old. The pupils of her eyes dilated, nearly erasing the iris. I reached her just as she seemed to tremble from head to foot. Her consummate control shattered. Swiftly I led her outside the room and held her as, torn with sobs, she fought to regain her habitually indestructible composure.

Finally, quieting, she whispered, "Did you see the one that looked like Pete?" I nodded. "And that darling little girl? And that adorable little blond boy?" I nodded. She was quiet now. "Did you ever see such smiles?"

I shook my head.

She took a deep breath and then another. "What happened to me? Why did I break into pieces like this?" She looked lost, bewildered.

"Maybe it was gratitude, honey." I said.

"Yes. That's what it was," she said. And then she whispered.

"Oh, I do thank you, Father."

There was another silence.

"Oh, Helen, how brave their mothers have to be!" she said.

A teacher came, then, to say the children were asking where the beautiful lady was. They wanted to "see" her.

As, Loretta, her control regained, stepped through the door, the beautiful little blond boy, about five or six, turned his face toward his teacher and asked, "Why did she cry? Did someone hurt her feelings?"

23

"No, darling," Loretta answered him. "Someone just gave me something I'm very grateful for!"

She bent over him and he sent his exploring, "seeing" hands over her face. She held tight to her smile while those tiny, sensitive fingers moved across her eyes, her mouth, her cheeks. Satisfied, his hands still cupping her chin, the little one again turned toward his teacher.

"She is *very* pretty," he said gravely. "Her smile is pretty, too!" He grinned happily. "No wonder somebody just gave her a nice present!"

The sweet sting of salt in our eyes lent, for that moment, just enough blindness for all of us to see as the little blind ones do. With the heart.

Of course, from the day we met, Loretta's knowledgeableness, her frankness, her generous credit-giving, her ability to express her convictions as incontrovertible fact and the high percentage of their accuracy were very impressive—and I was impressed.

I listened to her, glib, vocal and literal, tackle just about every subject. She was a girl with all the answers, the sure and quick advice, authoritatively delivered. She advised well and in accordance with principle, and always her advice was wrapped up very neatly in the precisely right quotation from her cherished quotations collection.

Inevitably, there were those who labeled her "opinionated." And there were those who said her every statement was a "pronouncement."

But, times without number, I had heard her favorite quotation, "You can't begin to know anything until you know you know nothing," and I knew that she believed it.

I admired her confidence in what she said, her standards of behavior, her disciplined professionalism and her deportment under any and all circumstances. There were example and inspiration in each. But, from all the times that I've been proud of her I sift the very special memory that sparkles for me.

When she came back, in 1955, after her long illness, she was bouncing with health, literally glowing with gratefulness. She rattled off enthusiastic recitations of what she'd learned in the long, long weeks of her hospitalization. Again, Loretta was her crisp, bright, authoritative self.

A few weeks later, back to work, she was giving an interview during her lunch hour. The interviewer said, "I understand you learned an awful lot from your illness."

She nodded happily.

"Just what did you learn?" he asked, pencil poised over his notebook.

The question seemed to stop her cold.

She just looked at him. She just looked at the man, not seeing him at all. Her eyes widened and I watched a kind of serenity grow in them. She seemed to be listening. I wondered what she was seeing—what she was hearing—as a long, long moment passed in an unaccustomed silence.

Where was Loretta's characteristically swift answer to any question?

And still the silence held!

Loretta looked down for a moment, moved the fork on her plate in an absent-minded sort of way, looked at her questioner again. Then she spoke, slowly, meditatively:

"I don't know," she said.

"I haven't proved it often enough yet," she added simply. "I do have to prove it over and over, don't I? Or I haven't really learned it, have I?"

I swallowed and I filed away, right then, a lot of the adjectives which had served me long, well and truthfully in my representation of Loretta Young. Words like brilliant, positive, articulate, clever, intelligent, smart—words grown synonymous with her name.

I remembered how often I'd heard her say, "You can't begin to know anything until you know you know nothing."

Now, I had seen and heard her come, with humility, simplicity and understanding, to the threshold of wisdom.

She'd reached that threshold with her sudden realization that knowledge is not merely a literal acceptance; not an intuitive or intellectual appreciation of truth, no matter how often and sincerely it is stated or recommended. Truth is not possessed, is not knowledge until it is practiced and proved over and over, and its use is habitual.

It was quiet again in that room. Loretta's interview was without any "pronouncements" and I heard the echo of the words of a man who lived in ancient Athens.

"Silence," this wise one had said, "is the fence around wisdom."

It was very heart-warming, after that day, to watch Loretta's method of expression grow more gentle, to hear her offer her opinions, self-labeled now, as what she *believed*. The quality of proclamation was gone. The high percentage of accuracy was not lessened but, now, her potential helpfulness was being controlled and directed.

It would no longer be just a happy accident in its effectiveness or in the realization of its purpose.

SALUTARE, VIATOR!

❦

CHAPTER ONE

The Wide, Wide World Outside

AFTER nine weeks of an inflexible "no non-family visitors" dictum, I was surprised when my day nurse told me Dr. Chess had okayed the visit requested by my representatives, Abe Lastfogel, Bert Allenberg and Norman Brokaw, of The William Morris Agency. I knew how busy these men are. It's a time-consuming drive from Beverly Hills to St. John's Hospital in Oxnard. This couldn't be a social call.

My nurse made much of the preparations for my first visitors. I must wear a ribbon in my hair. And lipstick.

As precisely punctual as a TV commercial, my visitors filed into the room, followed by Helen Ferguson, who's never along just for the ride. My suspicions that this visit was for an important business reason were confirmed.

They were sharing the burden of bad news! The starting date for the third production season of *The Loretta Young Show* was only two weeks away.

My greeting must have registered my apprehension because Helen's smile became brighter—deliberately reassuring.

My visitors wasted no time. Abe told me that even though my illness gave them the right to do so, Procter & Gamble did not want to cancel *The Loretta Young Show*. They'd rearranged the budget so the show could go on with guest hosts and hostesses and guest stars until my return, whenever that could be. P. & G. set no deadline.

Bert and Norman told me of the stars who'd already committed themselves to appear in my place: Barbara Stanwyck, Irene Dunne, Claudette Colbert, Merle Oberon, Rosalind Russell, Ann Sothern, Joseph Cotten, Van Johnson, Ricardo Montalban, Joan Fontaine.

They told me that Barbara Stanwyck, a dyed-in-the-wool TV hold-out, had been the first! Advised that *The Loretta Young Show* company and crew could be held together if enough top stars would sign to appear as hosts or hostesses, she'd said simply, "Tell me what to do and when and where to do it."

Two thirty-nine week seasons, meeting the endless creative, artistic and technical challenges of an anthology show forge a company, crew and star into a strong, close, working unit or scatter its parts into a nothing-at-all set-up.

thing. My entrance on *The Loretta Young Show* meant much more to me than any actress's entrance I'd ever made. Every time I opened that door I was a hostess greeting very welcome guests. It is a greeting which is very meaningful to me.

I signaled Helen to stay when Abe, Bert and Norman left. I'd just learned something. I had to say it and I could say it to her.

"*The Loretta Young Show* goes on. Without Loretta Young! That ought to teach me something."

"*The Loretta Young Show* is just waiting for you to open that door—and until whenever that is, a bench-full of eager pinch-hitters will vamp-until-you're-ready."

"There's a lesson in it though. . ."

"Then you'll sure learn it!" Helen spoke so positively I laughed! That was certainly an alien sound in *this* room.

"The things I've had to learn would fill a book!" I said.

"Well, why not?" Helen grinned, blew a kiss in my direction and walked to the door. She turned, grinned again and winked, as though we had just sealed some conspiratorial bargain!

I lay abed, smiling. Not much of a smile, maybe, but enough to be a valid symptom of the lift in my heart and I felt an energy I'd not known for weeks.

Gratitude isn't a burdening emotion.

Helen's "Well, why not?" kept bouncing around in my head and I discovered I didn't have a single "not" to answer it with. I discovered, instead, a veritable army of "whys."

This rich and wondrous acquaintance with gratitude was like

a bugler's reveille and the army of "whys" started to march.

I had to hurry to keep up with them and I bumped right into night-before-last.

I've always been scared to death of pain—afraid, even, to think of it. I wasn't afraid of anything else. Why was I so terrified of pain?

For long, long weeks this tiny hospital room was the arena in which pain and I held combat. At first, I was afraid I'd die of it. Then I was afraid I wouldn't.

There wasn't any day or night. The passing of time was marked by the gradations, the ebb and flow of pain. I discovered the indignities imposed by fear, the humiliations of helplessness. Sedatives held the pain at bay and blurred its sharpness, but I knew it wasn't through with me and I'd wait, terrified, for its return. The boundaries of my world had shrunk to the measurements of this room. The boundaries of my interest and concern were even smaller. Within them there was room only for pain, for fear and for the puppet they'd made of me.

This night the pounding of my heart thundered in the stillness of the hospital. I didn't pray—I begged.

"Why, God, why? What is thy will for me? Help me, Father, help me to learn. Help me to *learn!*"

For a long time my heartbeats hammered out all the sound

there was. Then, between heartbeats, I heard the sound of padded footsteps in the corridor. One—two—three—four steps; the whisper of a door hinge; silence. One—two—three—four steps; whisper of a door hinge; silence. Over and over, door after door.

I thought: behind every one of those doors someone is lying in a little room just like mine. Just as unwilling a tenant as I am.

Maybe just as scared?

I wondered about them. Why were they here? What was His will for them? What did they have to learn?

The moon's light filled the room and fell softly on the statue of the Blessed Mother, sent to me on Easter Sunday, weeks and weeks ago. In the sweet, soft light, she seemed to be smiling at me.

I wondered about her. I thought of the kind of pain she'd had to bear, of what she'd had to learn.

Had she cried, "Why? Why?"—even at the foot of the Cross?

I wondered about her Son. He'd endured agony beyond pain. Once, but only once, He did ask, "Why?"

We know that answer.

The moonlight offered other things in the room to my attention. A huge pile of letters, for one, typical of my daily mail every day since I'd been where I was. It came from friends I knew and from friends I'd never meet.

I wondered about all those people, all kinds of people in all kinds of places, who told me they were praying for me day after day. They didn't write like fans to a star.

They wrote as though they really cared about what happened to me as a human being!

My life had been spent in a very busy, fast-deadline world. It was a world with a heart—the most wonderfully generous, swift-to-help-everyone, charity-conscious kind of heart. But there'd never been time for me to learn much about the simple, patient, day-after-day, neighborly, unspectacular, individual and collective goodness of all the kind people outside the world I grew up in.

I thought of how often I'd felt alone. *All* alone. Against the world! Looking at those letters, I thought of all those who had helped me, one way or another, every step along the way. It was like whirling back through a veritable kaleidoscope, to remember all their brilliant directives, suggestions and advice. I saw how much I owed—and to how many!

All alone? Me? Was I an absent-minded idiot? I'd always considered myself very appreciative, but now I saw I'd taken an awful lot for granted. Until now, I'd never assembled *all* of those from whom I'd learned something into my gratefulness at one time.

The banners of my good fortune were very bright and crisp as the memory-parade I was master-minding passed in review.

It was a vast and motley crowd! It was practically everyone I'd ever met! It would take hours and hours and hours to call the roll.

The Wide, Wide World Outside

Well, I wasn't on any split-second schedule; I wasn't going anywhere. I had time to remember. I started the roll-call. I lined up my "teachers," relishing the examination of what I'd learned from each of them.

I'd walked with the very best of them—craftsmen, creative artists, those of beguiling loveliness, the extravagantly talented, the very wise, the strong in spirit, the dedicated religious. I'd walked with them, and with many who were none of these things. Sprinkled among my teachers, I discovered a goodly number from whom I'd have learned nothing at all—had they been my friends.

We certainly owe our enemies a great big thank-you, too, don't we? Was that why He told us to love them? I found I wanted to do it. And, I discovered that I could do it!

The color of dawn splashed my room. I wondered about what was going on in that wide, wide world outside. One thing I was sure of. This dawn was splashing its beauty all over that wide, wide world—on rich and poor, good and evil, the just and the unjust, on those at war and those at peace. It was dusting the darkness from cities, villages, rivers, oceans, mountains and valleys. This dawn was everywhere. It belonged to everyone. Take it or leave it.

I took it.

I let it have its way with me as though it were labeled: "Deliver this new day to Loretta Lewis in answer to her prayers."

I'm forever glad that I heard the sounds of that night—that I claimed that dawn.

When the sunrise came, it was, to me, a brilliant, majestic symbol of the brotherhood of man under the Fatherhood of God.

I wasn't scared any more.

When the pain came back, I didn't welcome it and I didn't like it. But I was able to tolerate it. Now, its disguise was quite transparent.

I wanted so much to hold onto the sweet, uncomplicated revelations of that night and that dawn. Of course that was as unrealistic as if I'd commanded time to halt in its orbit. I guess I knew I'd have to retrace the steps of my journey many, many times and for many, many reasons. To use what I'd learned, if I remembered all of it; to relearn my lesson, when I forgot any part of it. But each trip would be easier. I could get lost, of course. But having been that way once, I knew I could find it again.

I needed all I'd learned for what came next. Ten more weeks in the hospital. I clung to the memory of "my dawn" through surgery and recuperation and through weeks of disciplined convalescence after I left the hospital.

When, after nearly seven months away from the camera, for the season's nineteenth show, I opened the door, swirled through it and the crew applauded and cheered, "my dawn" was very bright, indeed. So were my tears. And theirs. The take was

ruined. My make-up was a mess. We were behind schedule
before we'd even started!

(Behind-schedule and over-budget are synonymous in TV.)

Who cared?

That's what a dawn can do for you!

CHAPTER TWO

Mamma

In common with many others in the varied branches of our profession, my academic education is sub-normal. Of course the law required that I be tutored at the studio and my teacher, Mrs. Holliday—God love her—was a realistic educator with a service-evaluation of the subjects she taught me. She boosted me through the quicksands of mathematics; she made me pass my grades, but after that was accomplished she didn't insist that I become a mathematician!

My ambition was certainly not anything I hid under a bushel, and I'm forever grateful that she slanted her teaching so that my academic education, such as it was, would serve me in my work. She didn't cram my scholastic inadequacies down my throat until they choked me into an inferiority complex.

So, all right, I can't spell. Well, I can always find someone who can! I've discovered good spellers don't mind helping a no-good speller out of a jam. All you have to do is ask, "How do you spell . . . ?" whatever it is, and have a quick hand on your pen, because good spellers spell fast!

Mrs. Holliday herself spelled me into passing even that subject. But she didn't ever let me off easy on rules and regulations. She was a martinet; no dawdling during lessons was permitted. I couldn't beguile her into letting me realize any truancy dreams I entertained. Not ever. That's how she taught me and why I learned to accept, without quibbling, the requiremnts of my job; the basic rules and regulations of professional deportment.

She knew that an actress must be sensitive to people; consciously and subconsciously, constantly aware of people. She knew that, if put to a contest, example rather than precept would teach me far more than it was her responsibility to grade me on. And she was a wonderful example. I loved her and I liked her. My appreciation of her example has grown to gratitude in the long time since I reached the end of my education as it was required by the law.

From Mrs. Holliday I learned that what I learned from her was not the end but the beginning of what I had to learn. She spent more time expanding the receptiveness of my mind than in stuffing it with a bloating accumulation of technical education-musts. She believed education should serve, not shackle. That certainly made us kin! She was the only teacher I had except, of course, the Sisters at the Sacred Heart Dominican Convent for one year and the Sisters at Ramona Convent for one other year. I really believe that if she'd insisted I receive a rubber-stamp education I'd have learned far less in the years afterward. As it is, nearly everyone I met, worked with, or read about was my teacher, one way or another.

"First and foremost," as Kathryn Forbes recorded, I remember Mamma. We've always spelled Mamma with two m's at our house—and I know I spell *that* right. From Mamma, by precept and example, I learned, I am still learning and will be, forever, learning.

When I was still a baby my father went away one day and never came back. Mamma didn't brood over it, or dramatize herself as an abandoned wife and mother. Mamma faced up to the fact. She was mother, father and family breadwinner. All of us kids thrived in the warmth and security of her devotion, and were unconcerned over the near-to-total-absence of money.

I was not quite four when Mamma moved all of us and all our worldly goods to Hollywood. Mamma's sister's husband, Uncle Trax, first arranged for my sisters, and then for me, to get work as child-extras in motion pictures, and Mamma opened a Boarding House.

What we kids earned at the studio was very welcome in the family kitty. Mamma was as selective of her paying guests and as solicitous of their comfort and convenience, once they passed her Kentucky-bred standards, as though they were her house guests, and in no way connected with anyone's livelihood.

So we never had much money. But we always had a rich abundance of all the things money can't buy. Love, trust, discipline, religious training. And we had lots and lots of fun!

Mamma prays as simply, constantly and confidently as she breathes. She could no more live without praying than she could if she ceased to breathe. As a result, she accepts each day's problems as calmly as she does the weather. Rain or shine. Her example in this fundamental, affirmative approach to living made me learn that the working-principle of trust in God can be applied to each and all of the infinite variations of circumstances. To simple, everyday problems as well as those of great or dramatic proportions.

I remember when I transferred from the first school to the other. At the first one we had to wear uniforms. At the second one we didn't.

I had the uniforms. Our funds being what they were, the cost of the uniforms was enough that, having them, I had no dresses. No problem, I thought. I simply wore my uniforms to the new school. They marked me as different, set me apart. Some of my classmates made me realize this fact and then I did have a problem. The day that one of the girls asked, "Haven't you any dresses at all?" her tone really shriveled my pride and I came home crying.

I sobbed my story to Mamma. She put her arms around me, but without any excess of sympathy. She said firmly: "Now see here, Gretchen. Whatever you wear is always neat. It is always clean. The other childrn may have very fine clothes, but they cannot be more immaculate than your uniforms. It's nice to have fine clothes, but it's not important. It *is* important to be clean. 'Cleanliness is next to Godliness.'"

As far as Mamma was concerned, that was the end of it.

Of course her arms were comforting, but there was no non-sense in her attitude. She expected me to adjust to the fact that the uniforms had to be worn. She made me feel proud of their cleanness. She made me proud to be different. And I know that this gave me an independence which has helped me in my work and in my life.

Like most of us, I've learned that getting a part of what you want gives you a pretty high batting average, and leaves you plenty to struggle for. If you win everything you've set your heart on, what's left to want? But I wasn't always that bright about it. I've never forgotten the time—I think I must have been a quick fifteen—when I was positive the world would come to an end because I didn't get a full-length ermine coat I wanted.

I was doing marvelously well in pictures, I thought. My salary had jumped from $60 to $100 to $250 a week! At last Mamma decided it was time we could look at fur coats. I was walking on air as we trotted downtown to a furrier's. "You're not getting it now, Gretchen," Mamma warned me. "It's to be your Christmas present."

I had my heart set on a full-length ermine wrap. Nothing, just nothing else would do. I put one on and posed and preened possessively, like the peacock I was. Mamma said: "Don't be silly. That's much too old for you."

She selected a dabby, short ermine stole. I couldn't have cared less for anything. But, knowing Mamma, who often, when she'd said I couldn't have a certain thing, presented it to me as a gift for Christmas or my birthday, I "modeled" the little old ermine stole and set my patience the happy task of awaiting my gorgeous Christmas present. I humored Mamma by pretending I didn't expect the long ermine coat—ever. I didn't want to spoil her surprise.

I didn't.

When Christmas finally came, there it was—the beautiful, ribbon-wrapped box from the furrier. For me! I almost tore the box apart in my happy excitement. And was I proud! So proud and so pleased that my patience was to have its reward.

I lifted the last layer of tissue paper, my eyes eager to feast themselves on my dream-coat. They gazed upon, instead, something I simply could not believe.

Mamma

That dinky little ermine stole was the only thing in the box.

"Mamma!" I screamed. Then I burst into tears of total abject misery. My sobs rent the air. I felt betrayed! Mamma and my sisters failed to persuade me that the coat I had set my heart on was "an old lady's coat." I succeeded in completely ruining the holiday for the whole family. I carried on, inconsolably, until even the Christmas tree looked little and mean and much too bright in this home filled with my woe.

Today, I wonder why Mamma didn't spank me. I'd never deserved it more. But she didn't. She maintained the calm of her wisdom—her inflexible, wise, patient calm. She was right. She knew it. And she could bear whatever being right thrust upon her.

I've set my heart on a lot of things since, of course, but whenever it gets real set on something, deep inside me I can hear the crackle of tissue paper and I get myself braced, *if* I heed the warning sound, for disappointment. Wouldn't you?

Just after I entered my teens I suddenly entertained an insatiable enthusiasm for the delightful habit of criticizing others. I wasn't alone in the practice—and there are those who'd say it was just part of a normal teenster's "development."

Mamma thought otherwise.

I had a very special target for my criticism. Her name was

Sylvia. She was thirteen, too. She was pretty, always happy and carefree, and as quick as Bob Hope with the witty comeback, the bright retort. She bubbled along as though every day and everyone were just too, too wonderful. She was a little bit of a thing. Cute, and grinning all the time. I just couldn't stand her.

It was pretty disgusting to see how popular she was with everybody.

I was particularly repetitive of one point in my endless criticism. I always wound up with, "How on earth anyone as little as she is can be so popular is beyond me!"

One day, Mamma called me into the kitchen and closed the door.

"Why do you dislike Sylvia so intensely?" she asked.

"I don't dislike her, Mamma," I protested. "She just bores me, that's all. And how on earth anyone as little as . . .?"

Mamma stopped me right there.

"Dear, you know height has nothing to do with popularity!" She was really quite stern about it. She repeated, "Why do you dislike Sylvia? Tell the truth, Gretchen."

The command confused me. I honestly didn't know "why?" I shook my head in bewilderment and Mamma let me have it.

"You're jealous of her, Gretchen."

Shocked, I started to protest, but Mamma would have none of it.

"That's the truth. You're jealous of her. Now, learn this. Your jealousy will not hurt her. It is hurting you. Every time you criticize her you're feeding your envy. Envy's ugly and it ill-becomes you, Gretchen."

I felt as though Mamma'd thrown me to the lions! Why, Mamma was on Sylvia's side!

"I'd suggest that you make a determined effort to say something nice about Sylvia whenever you feel compelled to talk about her." She said "suggest" but she was giving a command.

Then Mamma's eyes twinkled. "I'd make a very special effort, Gretchen, since she's almost your only subject of conversation."

I decided it wasn't a time to argue with Mamma. I decided it would be a pretty good idea to give her instructions a try.

It wasn't easy, but I managed it. Before long Sylvia and I were fast friends. She was much more fun than any of the other girls—anybody with any sense at all could see why Sylvia was so popular!

So many of my memories and so much that I've learned are stitched with the deceptively fragile thread of Mamma's wisdom. I never cease to wonder at the delicacy of those stitches. Mamma's wisdom is steel-strong, tested and tempered. That it seems like a thread instead of a rope is because of the delicacy, the feather-lightness, the subtleness of Mamma's use of it.

There were times when her subtlety was downright bewildering—until I discovered that those were the times when she knew I'd have to learn my way out of a lesson with as little help as possible.

When I was fourteen, I had a terrific crush on a boy. He seemed to know I was on earth, but he certainly didn't show any signs of thinking I was anything special. I was thinking of disciplining myself to accept my fate, of resigning myself to a lifetime of unrequited love when, the day before Christmas, he came to the house and tossed a gift-wrapped package to me.

"It's your present," he said. I was thrilled speechless.

He said, "Open it."

It was the most gorgeous, exquisite, divine, adorable, heavenly-beautiful evening bag in the whole world! I was sure it must have cost a fortune!

I was ecstatic! He *did* think I was pretty special! I couldn't take my eyes from this momentous proof of his devotion.

"Oh, you shouldn't have," I breathed. "You shouldn't have."

"But I wanted to," he said.

From my perch on cloud nine I said again, "Oh, but you shouldn't have."

He said again, "But I wanted to."

And again I said, "Oh, but you shouldn't have."

He looked dashed, bewildered, disappointed. All of a sudden, without another word, he left! He didn't even say goodbye. And he slammed the door!

I was stunned. "What on earth's the matter with him?" I appealed to Mamma.

She gave me one of her long, level looks. "Well, Gretchen, you're right. He shouldn't have!"

I could tell she wasn't on my side. Why? I went back over everything that had happened from the time he arrived until the door slammed. It was too deep for me!

Finally, I got it.

That's how I learned that a gift must be received gratefully and honestly. Unless it is, the giving of it—the gift itself—is ruined. Giving and receiving are like two pieces of a coin. If they aren't matched, neither has any value.

I had been so preoccupied with my own selfish delight that I didn't even share it with the one who was responsible for it. No wonder Mamma let me find my own way out of that bog!

That's what I mean about the delicacy of the thread of her wisdom.

How I wish that boy could have known that he gave me the absolutely unforgettable Christmas present of my life. The lesson I learned because of it is one of the few I had to learn only once.

Once in a while I learned one of Mamma's lessons from observation. Or was it eavesdropping?

I remember the night one of my sisters came storming home from a high school dance. Her date was the football hero of the school and she'd been quite queenly about this fact all week.

She wasn't queenly now. She was plain, hopping mad. She tore into Mamma's room and launched into a non-stoppable harangue against her date. *He* was a hero? He was not! He was a moron, a goon, a JERK!

Her evening had been a total flop instead of the social triumph she'd expected as the gridiron hero's date. Said "JERK," from what I could hear from my room down the hall, had spent the entire evening talking *football* with another boy! The two of them had sat, right beside her, and talked FOOTBALL, FOOTBALL, FOOTBALL! Her date didn't even ask her to dance! And, of course, none of the other boys would ask her while their hero was sitting with her. And she would never, never go out with him again! And she had told him so! Just let him ask her! Just let him!!

She finally ran out of breath.

I heard Mamma ask, "Are you sure it wouldn't have been a nicer evening if you'd shown some interest in the conversation?"

"But I'm not interested in football!" my sister protested.

"I thought all your excitement about this date was because he's the school's best football player."

"Well, yes. That's what made him the best date. *That's* why I was excited. I told you that, Mamma. It wasn't because I'm interested in *football!*"

Mamma's voice was very gentle.

"But he is."

"But he had a date with me!"

"I know—he must have been very disappointed in you."

Mamma

"He must have been disappointed in *me?"* My sister's voice was shocked, incredulous.

"Why not, dear? It certainly can't be any secret that he likes football. How could he know that you don't? Of course, you won't see him again. But the same thing can happen to you again, and it will—whenever you have a date with a boy who isn't interested only in you. You must learn to be interested in whatever subject your date is interested in. That is, if you expect anyone to be interested in dating you more than once."

That did it. There wasn't even a tiny peep out of my sister. She never came home in a tizzy after that, though. And she always had scads of beaux after that and dates galore.

The word "charm" hadn't entered the conversation I overheard. But, listening, I know I got my very first lesson in how to acquire it. Actually, what Mamma projected was the oldest, the wisest, the most practical rule there is—for charm —for anything.

No wonder it's called the Golden Rule.

Mamma's example has been a wonderful lesson-giver, too. As a Catholic, Mamma believes absolutely that she must "hate the sin but love the sinner." She doesn't dramatize this requirement of her religion. She practices it simply, honestly, directly.

She sees nothing extraordinary in any behavior inspired by her obedience to it, and she gave me a memorable example of its practice when we were on a visit to Paris.

We were having dinner at a beautiful outdoor café in the park. I can't remember how it came about that a young, but unmistakable lady-of-the-evening attached herself to us. She sat down at our table and she and Mamma were soon in deep conversation. Even though Mamma knew we were going to be late for an appointment, my subtle signals weren't getting through. Finally, I gave up being subtle. I leaned over and whispered into Mamma's ear and I identified our visitor's profession.

Very calmly Mamma set about concluding the conversation, apologizing for our need to keep an appointment. Her goodbye to our guest was sweet, warm, friendly.

We were hardly out of earshot when I started, reproachfully, "Now, *really,* Mamma . . ." I got no further.

"I'm very sure you're wrong, Gretchen," Mamma said firmly. "That poor little thing has a great many problems. I do hope I was able to give her some helpful advice."

Mamma's no softie, either. Once, when we were in Rome we received an official invitation to call on Mussolini. Mamma held to some very definite views about Mussolini's regime. She disapproved of many of his dictatorship tactics and she considered the presence of his Black Shirts an unwarranted intimidation of the gay and friendly Italian people.

She read the invitation very thoughtfully. Then she said, "I don't think the man's a gentleman. I don't think we will call upon him." And we didn't.

The consternation and the concern of many of our friends

and of members of the international set couldn't have meant less to Mamma.

With this example of uncomplicated honesty right in the family, is it any wonder I've learned to stand firm—if I'm sure I'm standing on a *principle*?

CHAPTER THREE

My Star and I

Of course it was Mamma who both stopped my career and crystalized my determination to resume it.

I'd thought of myself as a great big motion picture star from the time I was six. I didn't like being lost in a crowd of kid extras, so I started to pretend I was a star and, from somewhere, I always got some idea which kept me from being lost—at least in my own estimation. I ran faster than the other kids if we were supposed to run in a scene; I lagged if we were supposed to walk; I sat down if all the rest were standing; I stood if all the rest were seated. I simply moved against the crowd and if all it got me was a reprimand from the director, well, that's better than no attention, isn't it?

The Things I Had to Learn

Maybe it was my acting like a big star all over the place at home that got us all enrolled at the convent where for stellar, individualistic tactics there was no possibility of reward and any inspirations in that category had to be stifled.

Very often I felt lonely and at night I'd tip-toe to my sister Bet's room and crawl into bed with her.

It never even occurred to me to resist Mamma's decision. I simply coped with it by withdrawing into dreams of what and where I'd be when I'd survived it and this kind of learning. I learned to sew. I learned the inflexibility of rules and I learned that gentle tones and good manners, as exemplified by the Sisters, are not the badge of a milquetoast.

Arithmetic! All it meant to me was that figures could become unlimited amounts. Add, I could. Subtract, I could not. Multiply? I'll say! But not just figures—I multiplied my dreams into all the things I wanted. All the things I'd get when I was a *star!*

My scrubby little school papers were as good as I could make them with my head so crowded with bright plans for tomorrow, but they guaranteed I'd not be any scholarship-threat. When I was particularly close to a not-passing mark I'd really cram to toe-over that barrier. I didn't intend to get stuck in the same old grade forever.

I comforted myself with the poet's advice to "let who will be clever," and while I wasn't the smartest in my class I was a very good girl, indeed. I provided no menace to the scholastically ambitious ones—and they provided no challenge to me.

The between-vacations months of my second convent year

passed very slowly. They passed even more slowly after the January 6th that I was twelve years old. June did get around, though, finally!

It was Pol and Bet who got work in the studios right away. And better parts than ever before. It took all I'd learned from the Sisters' good example to hold my impatience in leash.

I dreamed my dreams and sat by the telephone. Ours was the fastest answered phone in town! And one day the call did mean something. Even though it wasn't a call for me.

"Hello," I said.

"This is Mervyn LeRoy—First National," the man's voice said. "Let me speak to Polly Ann Young."

"Polly Ann's working, Mr. LeRoy," I reported.

"We've got a part for her. Shoots day after tomorrow."

"Pol's on location, Mr. LeRoy. She won't be back till next week."

I took a deep breath. So what if Pol was four years older? I was taller!

"Won't *I* do, Mr. LeRoy?"

Well, I'd said it.

"Who are *you?*" Mr. LeRoy's voice seemed to be smiling.

"I'm Gretchen and I'm an actress, too, and I'm available. Day after tomorrow, that is."

"Hmm," Mr. LeRoy remarked. "Hmm," he repeated. Then there was silence. I let it be that way. Finally, Mr. LeRoy said, "Come on out to the studio, Gretchen. Since you're an actress, too, let's have a look at you."

In a tone as majestic as Ethel Barrymore's, my mouth dry

as cotton and the buzz of triumph in my head, I made the most momentous speech of my life.

"Yessir!" I said.

I ran all the way to the bus.

It was the slowest bus I ever rode on and at each bus transfer—it took three buses to get to First National, way out in Burbank—I had to wait so long I thought they'd have finished making the picture before I ever got to the studio.

But, if you can trust a clock, I was there in less than an hour. Mr. LeRoy couldn't have been nicer but he told his assistant to put me into "the kids' scene."

I wasn't going to get Pol's part after all. Even with only four silly years between Pol and me! "Well, Rome wasn't built in a day." I told the lump in my throat. When it didn't go away, I gave it a stern reminder of how long I'd waited for *anything* in the studios. That did away with it.

I went out to the set, appraised the other "kids" in the scene, and watched the star—Colleen Moore.

She really was a great *BIG* star.

I watched her like a hawk.

She wasn't very beautiful, but she was a star. She wasn't very elegant, but she was a star. She wasn't very graceful, but she was a star. She wasn't aloof and queenly, but she was a star. She didn't even have eyes the same color—she had one blue eye and one brown eye. But she was a *star!*

I had to know *why*.

I stared and stared and wondered. She was like no other star I'd ever seen and I knew she was the biggest star in Hollywood right then and everybody knew she had practically a million dollars and she'd earned it all herself!

Well, what was she? What she wasn't was very clear. But, what *was* she?

She was like electricity! She sparkled with enthusiasm. She held a happiness about her. She talked to everybody and anybody and she let anybody tell her any old idea anybody thought up and she listened as though she cared!

And, I noticed, she checked every idea with Mr. LeRoy. He was her gag-man.

It was too deep for me. The only one I cared about listening to was the director. So—I listened to him.

When the day's work ended, we kids were told to be back on the set in the morning. I'd get two days' checks!

Just before lunch that second day I noticed some men talking with Miss Moore. I thought they were looking at me and I wondered if I'd thought up one too many against-the-crowd things to do in the scenes I'd been in.

I was scared.

But they went away and I hadn't been fired or even scolded, so maybe they hadn't been talking about me after all.

Late in the afternoon the assistant director told me the front office had sent a man to tell him to tell me to report to Mr. Al Rockett, the head of the studio, when we finished working.

I *had* done something wrong!

I rushed up to Mr. Rockett's office as soon as we were dismissed.

"We're going to put you under contract, Gretchen," he said.

"Your name won't do. Colleen Moore's changed it to Loretta. All right with you?"

I must have agreed somehow, because he said: "Fine. We'll get the papers ready for your mother to sign."

He smiled. It was a nice smile.

"You're a lucky kid," he said. "Thanks to Colleen Moore."

Colleen Moore hadn't even spoken to me. The interview was over and I hadn't opened my mouth.

I triple-bus rode my way home. At least, I guess I did. I was in such a state I don't remember. But how else did I get there?

Mamma said, when I'd told her my news: "How nice of Miss Moore. She must be well-born. Iron your other dress, Gretchen. You must be nice and clean."

Iron my dress! My star-dreams were taking over. Ironing was no chore for a star!

It seemed a pretty good idea to do the chore though—just in case.

I didn't work with Colleen Moore again until I was thirteen and I was given the part of an older girl in *Naughty, But Nice*. My adult career had started.

I learned a lot of things from Colleen Moore.

I learned a lot of things *about* Colleen Moore, too.

She'd been as determined to be a star as I was. Since she was a kid, too. She'd had to overcome a lot of things because she wasn't just as pretty as a picture and she worked, worked, worked. She never complained, she was always excited with each new scene. And even when things got all snarled up she kept her pixie-like excitement sprinkling its enthusiasm all over the problem—whatever it was.

She always saw things no one else ever saw. I wasn't the only one! Why, she believed in Mervyn LeRoy when he was only a struggling young comic who didn't get many jobs, but he always danced and joked at all the Benefits. She saw him at one of them. She made the studio hire him as her gagman. And, in time, she insisted the studio let him direct her pictures!

Colleen Moore *loved*.

She loved work and people and fun and beautiful things, like ivories and miniatures and silver and china. She loved the lore of the Irish. She loved—and she believed—fairy tales, and all the tales of the pixies and leprechauns. She believed in fairy princesses and fairy godmothers. She loved, and believed, everything that was lovely.

One day, when she was very rich, she built something she'd always dreamed of—the loveliest doll house the world ever saw. It was a Fairy Princess' castle.

Its furnishing were priceless miniatures. Some were of gold and silver and precious stones. The chandelier in its great hall sparkled as it did because it was made of diamonds and emeralds that had once been in her grandmother's necklace!

For years Colleen Moore's Doll House was exhibited in cities all over the country, and she donated the proceeds of millions of paid admissions to charities in every one of those cities. Colleen Moore knew how to share her dreams!

A few years ago, she gave the Doll House to the Museum

of Science and Industry in Chicago. A special room was constructed to display it and to insure its preservation.

There's never been anything in the world like Colleen Moore's Doll House.

There's never been anyone in the world like Colleen Moore, either!

After *Naughty, But Nice,* I didn't see her for a long, long time. Having been my rocket, once I was launched, she let me orbit on my own.

One day, when I was making *The Farmer's Daughter,* Helen Ferguson was on the set. While we were talking between scenes Helen glanced across the stage. Her face lit up. She left me in the middle of a sentence and ran to a group of visitors. She came back with the lady member of the group.

"Loretta, you know Mrs. Hargrave . . ."

Looking at Colleen Moore, warmed by the magic of that wonderful pixie-grin of hers, I learned that day what "beauty is from within" really means.

Mrs. Homer P. Hargrave of Chicago is beautiful! She is, and she shows that she is, a fulfilled woman—a really successful *woman.*

She had what it took to become a big star. She had what it took to make a great deal of money. She had what it took to quit at the top. She said she'd retire when she'd made a million dollars. She had what it took to do what she'd said. She made the million. She retired. She moved away from Hollywood. She married widower Homer P. Hargrave, member of a distinguished brokerage firm in Chicago. She became

My first photograph, taken with Mamma (Gladys Royal Young), in Salt Lake City

Mamma (now Mrs. Gladys Royal Belzer) and I in 1959.

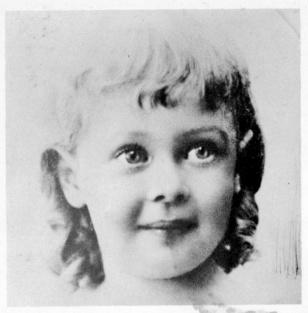

This is how I looked at four, when I started work in Hollywood as a child extra.

In my school uniform at Ramona Convent, Alhambra, California.

With Colleen Moore in *Naughty But Nice* (1927), my first "adult" role. I'm the teenager at the left with a sideburn curl.

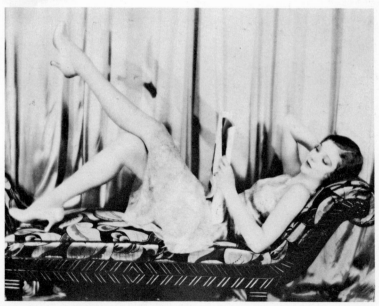

As a Wampas Baby Star, about 1929.

TWO OF MY "GLITTERING" ROLES, FROM WHICH I BROKE AWAY TO FREE LANCE.

Courtesy of 20th Century Pictures, Inc.

With Sir George and Lady Arliss in *The House of Rothschild* (1934).

With Tyrone Power in *Suez* (1938).

Courtesy of 20th Century-Fox

A role I was afraid to play—Katie, in *The Farmer's Daughter* (1947)—
but for which I won an Oscar.

With Clark Gable in *Key to the City* (1950).

MY ALL-TIME FAVORITE ROLE—
SISTER MARGARET MARY in *COME TO THE STABLE*
(1949)

Courtesy of 20th Century-Fox

Courtesy of 20th Century-Fox

On my visit to The Lighthouse of the New York Association of the
Blind. The doll played a small but important part in *The Bishop's
Wife,* the picture in which I co-starred with Cary Grant and David
Niven.

With Loretta Variety
Young, the baby
abandoned in a Phil-
adelphia theater during
the Variety Clubs
International
convention in 1951,
and adopted by the
Philadelphia Tent of
Variety Clubs.

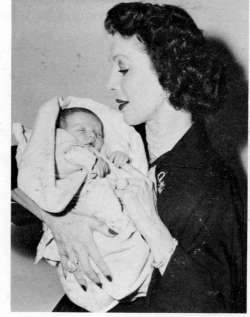

One of my proudest moments—the night I won an Oscar.

a mother to his children, a vital part of Chicago society, a tireless worker in its charity organizations.

She did all these things. But it's what she *is* that stamped the special loveliness upon her eager, happy face.

She's quite a person. It shows. It glows.

It is something very beautiful to see.

Our visit on the set that day was short but sweet.

It was revealing, too. I'd never been told (and I'd never asked) why Miss Moore wanted the studio to sign me on that long ago day. That she *had* was enough! When I read in the paper that she'd named me Loretta after her Patron Saint, I didn't question that, either.

Helen Ferguson and Colleen were very old friends; they'd once been kid-extras, too (when they were thirteen and fourteen), at the Essanay Studio in Chicago. This day, Helen asked Colleen the "whys" I never had.

Colleen told the story as though it had nothing to do with me, and such is her gift of story-telling, that listening, even I forgot that it had.

She told it as though it were a fairy-tale.

Come to think of it, it really was like one, wasn't it?

"Well, once upon a time, when I was a little girl, I lived in Tampa, Florida," Colleen said. "They told the story there, of the Princess Loreta who, long ago, lived in a castle of ivory and gold. She was kidnapped, one stormy evening, by the bandit Gasparillo, who swept her up into his arms and sped away with her on his jet-black horse. The drawings of the Princess Loreta in the book were of wondrous beauty and the Princess herself was as beautiful as the loveliest dream.

"The Christmas I was eight, I was given a doll—the most beautiful doll I'd ever seen and she looked so much like the pictures of the Princess Loreta that I couldn't name her anything else.

"Loreta, my doll, was part of the heart of my childhood. She was, to me, the symbol of all beauty and loveliness.

"One day, long later, I saw a little girl—among a lot of little girls—on one of my sets. At first, I thought I knew her. Then I wasn't sure.

"This little girl didn't play around between scenes with the others. She had huge gray eyes and seemed to be watching everything. Studying everyone. She listened as though she were the only one the director was talking to when he told all the kids what to do in a scene. Between scenes she kept herself alone. She always stood near the director and his assistant. She didn't get under foot. She was all business. She was always there when she was wanted. And, very deliberately, in each scene she was in, she always did something different from all the others.

"I understood this child. I studied her face. I saw the good bones beneath its child-soft contours. I knew, then, why she'd looked familiar to me. She looked like my doll! I did what I had to do.

"I called the front office. I said that I had found a star. I said for them to hurry to the set and see for themselves what I had found!

"When they got there I showed them.

" 'You've got to put her under contract,' I told them. 'She will be a great beauty! She will be a star.'

"They were polite, unexcited. Couldn't they *see*? Finally, one of them said, 'But her name! Gretchen's too dutchy.'

"Good heavens! Was that any kind of an obstacle?

" 'Change it,' I said.

" 'Change it?' The man made it sound impossible.

"She looked like my doll. So, she looked—of course she did —like the picture of the lovely, lovely Princess.

" 'Call her Loreta!' I said.

" 'Too foreign,' someone said, after a long time of thinking about it.

"It was time for me to tell—not ask.

" 'All right. All right! Add another T. Call her Loretta. But, for heaven's sake, sign her!' "

Colleen stopped speaking. She'd taken me, somehow, so out-of-myself that I wanted and waited to hear the end of the story!

I started to ask, "And did they?" "And they did!" I said instead. I said it so earnestly that we all laughed!

Then Colleen said, "I think—I do hope——she lived happily ever after!"

It wasn't a question. But I gave her my answer anyway.

"She's lived a great deal of happiness, Colleen. She's not a fairy-princess, though. I don't think she'd want to be. But for all the happiness she'd never have known without your kindnesses, believe me, she's ever-after grateful."

"Pooh!" said Mrs. Hargrave of Chicago. "It *had* to happen to that child! Bones don't lie! And, sooner or later, that she was a pro had to show, too."

I looked at her—at her face fairly shining with good will. And I knew that Colleen Moore's example of what makes a very great lady would certainly live happily ever-after!

❊

CHAPTER FOUR

Be—and Believe

I was a very-positive-about-everything-very-impatient-thirteen. I'll say! Caution and patience were words somebody else could have. They were not for me.

Wait. Wait. Wait. For what? *Why?*

I'd already been waiting over half of my whole life!

It was years and years ago that I was six. Then I had decided, set my goal and declared my destination.

I was going to be a motion picture star.

Months ago I had selected my model. She was gorgeous, glamorous, rich and famous. Colleen Moore was something special and wonderful but she just wasn't my idea of a movie

star. She was something so extraordinary no one could dupli-
cate her anyhow. My model was exactly my idea, and ideal,
of a Movie Queen. She was beautiful, graceful, charming,
gracious, and she lived in a world of grandeur and adula-
tion.

But she couldn't live forever, could she? Somebody had to
take her place, someday. That somebody could be me. That
somebody should be me. I decided that somebody would
be me! I worked like crazy to be ready for that someday.

I haunted her sets when she was working, trailed her all
over the lot, goggled my eyes out studying her on the screen,
spent hours practically glued to my mirror, practicing her
gestures and her slow, alluring smile. I copied her make-up,
her hairdo, her mannerisms, her voice, her walk. And, to the
absolute outside limit of my gnat-size budget, I copied her
clothes.

I was a real smug smarty-pants when people began to notice.
It was beautiful music to my ears whenever anyone said, "Why,
you look just like Corinne Griffith!" or, "Why, for a minute I
thought you were Corinne Griffith!" So far: all A's on my
report card.

That's the way things were on the day Al Rockett, head
of the studio, said: "Come to my office, Loretta. I've been
watching you."

I was dizzy with triumph!

While Mr. Rockett talked on the phone, my triumph pro-
pelled me into deciding which dressing room I wanted in
Star Row, and exactly how I'd have it redecorated and re-

furnished, and I decided I'd have a snazzy, all-white car, an all-white wardrobe and the longest, fullest whitest ermine coat in town.

Mr. Rockett finished talking and I willed myself away from the contemplation of the dazzlingly beautiful panorama of my stellar future to listen, with corinne-griffith-like graciousness, to what he was to tell me.

"Child," he said, "no matter how hard you try—you'll never be anything but a second-rate Corinne Griffith. Why don't you try to make something first-rate out of Loretta Young?"

His words roared like thunder in my head. His shocking, incredible words cut my dreams to shreds. They smashed my star-bright world and scattered it into little pieces so that it was nothing. Nothing at all.

I sat there in the rubble of it. There wasn't even any breath left in me.

Through the blur of tears which I would not let spill, I saw Mr. Rockett smile the kind of tender smile a grown-up gives only to a child. It was a smile I neither acknowledged nor returned.

He seemed to be waiting for something. He couldn't expect me to thank him, could he?

I groped for the raveled remnants of my young dignity and managed, "I shall consider your question, Mr. Rockett."

"Do that, Gretchen," he said. "But first—go wash your face."

He grinned and held his hand out across his desk. But, my chin a mile in the air, I tore blindly out of his office, ran straight through the studio gates, and when I got home, straight to my mirror.

My mirror reported: one face, tear-streaked, mascara-smeared, mouth drooping with self-pity. I stared, hypnotized, at that gulping mess.

All of a sudden I understood Mr. Rockett.

He wasn't trying to smash what I'd built so earnestly. He knew I had to build something not so fragile, something strong enough to stand, and withstand, the tests and obligations of my ambition.

I washed my face, changed my clothes, went back to the studio and waited for two hours until Mr. Rockett could see me again.

"I came back to thank you, Mr. Rockett," I said.

He stood up and now he grinned—grown-up to grown-up. I grabbed his hand, shook it real hard and grinned right back at him.

"How lovely you look, Loretta!" he said. Then he said, very soberly, "You *are* going to be a star. Someday."

"I am, Mr. Rockett? I *am?"*

"It won't be easy. We'll help. But most of all—and always —you'll have to be yourself, believe in yourself. Remember that, Gretchen, when it's real tough and real lonely. Be yourself. Believe in yourself. Make yourself responsible. I know you'll say your prayers all the way to the top. And when you get there, Loretta, well, you'll need them there more than ever."

He grinned again. The interview was ended.

"Remember, now: Be yourself."

Be—and Believe

"Oh, I will, Mr. Rockett." I promised eagerly. "I will!"

A lot of years later, I'd been a star for quite a while, and thirteen-year-old ambitious kids were copying my make-up, my hairdo, my manner and my walk. After eight years of a modest-salaried, yearly-options deal, the studio offered me a straight five-year-no-option-two-million-dollar contract.

You'll feel as all my advisers did when I didn't grab the nearest pen and sign all seven copies of that contract before the studio had a chance to change its mind!

I wanted to grab that pen.

What stopped me?

I felt I was in a sparkling, tinsel-lined, successful box-office career-rut. I saw it getting five years deeper. I believed I could play roles of substance and meaning. The frothy, exquisitely-costumed roles I'd done for so long had immobilized me in glittering, cobwebby glamour—like a bisque-bride on the top of a wedding cake.

When I'd bedecked myself to copy Corinne Griffith, Mr. Rockett sent me home to wash my face. Now a studio-bedecked, pretty-puss-clothes-horse, *I* wanted to "wash my face."

Some said: "You fool! You willful fool!" Those who loved me very much reminded: "The greatest pride goeth before a fall."

What *did* possess me? Why did I pick this, of all times, to want to free-lance? Every box-office star was under contract. Plum assignments go to contract-stars. Where could I get anything better than at my own studio?

Was I willful? Was I prideful? Was I?

"Real tough and real lonely," Mr. Rockett had said.

"Real tough." Trying to explain what only time could prove. "Real tough." To withstand the pleading arguments of those with nothing to gain, who just didn't want me to make a mistake.

"Real lonely." I'll say it was.

I prayed for Guidance. Very urgently.

Myron Selznick, my agent, the one who really did stand to lose if I didn't sign, asked, "Loretta, do you really know how much money you're turning down?" I answered very slowly, desperately afraid of his misunderstanding, "But—it's only money." He had a poker-face. The silence that followed was unlike any other silence I've ever known. Waiting in it, even my heart stood still. He ended it.

"Okay. I'll believe in you! And just as much as you believe in yourself. C'mon, Loretta! We're going free-lancing!"

Well, I didn't work at all for nine months! But, after that there were studios where I could get the parts I wanted on a free-lance basis and, eventually at the salary Myron was brave enough to demand. And, thank God, there were enough of them—year after year.

Way back in 1947, Dore Schary sent me a script, "Katie." I read it, and went to the studio to tell him I couldn't do it.

"Why can't you do it, Loretta?"

"One, I'm not Swedish. Two, I don't have an accent. Three, I'm not a blonde."

Dore said: "Let's start backwards. You can bleach your hair. [I never have.] You can learn an accent."

"Southern, maybe, on account of Mamma. But Swedish? No. I couldn't."

"Couldn't, Loretta? Aren't you an actress? Don't you believe in yourself enough to learn an accent?"

Now why did Mr. Rockett have to get into the act?

There wasn't a split-second between Mr. Schary's question and my answer.

"All right. I'll play 'Katie.' I'll bleach my hair. I'll have the best Swedish accent this side of Stockholm!"

Ruth Roberts, who coached Ingrid Bergman out of her accent, coached me into mine. I loved playing Katie. And I'm very grateful to her.

You see, "Katie," the seventy-fourth picture of my real adult career, became *The Farmer's Daughter,* and gave me the biggest surprise—the incomparable thrill—of my life!

A seasoned spectator at Academy Awards presentations, I was cloud-borne at this one to the winners' spotlight, and Frederic March put a golden, shining Oscar into *my* hand!

I didn't feel alone in that spotlight. I wasn't. Invisible, but very present were Dore Schary, Mr. Rockett, and believe it or not, in the spotlight's long shadow behind me, there was a thirteen-year-old girl with a fresh-washed face.

In 1949 there was a new thing called Television, to which my agency and advisers were adamantly opposed as a performance medium for their "top" clients. Anyway, I couldn't have cared less. It didn't have anything to do with me. I was on the full picture-making schedule my husband approved: not more than four pictures in any twenty-four months—three, he thought, was even better.

We got our first TV set. I was enchanted with the recurrent presence, in our home, of Kate Smith and Ted Mack; the boys could hardly wait until Hopalong Cassidy time each evening; Judy had her special-precious programs, too, and Tom sat smug, sure and silent as the family gatherings began to center about that TV screen. (Tom's an advertising executive—which explains the way he sat.)

I was sure that Television would grow. That in time, and somehow, the whole wide world would shrink itself into little screens in living rooms all over the earth. I was possessive of everything I saw on ours.

By 1950 I wanted to go "visiting." "Like Kate Smith," I said.

Everyone howled! "You're no Kate Smith, Loretta. You're an actress!"

They thought I was crazy, believing in TV the way I did. I thought they were ostriches.

I wanted to "visit;" to do something—well, helpful—like, for instance: I'd lived by quotations, practically all my life. Why couldn't I share what they'd done for me?

My agency, studying warily this johnny-come-lately-to-show-business, told me NBC wanted to make a deal. It was my turn to howl.

"Go ahead!" I told them.

"Why rush, Loretta? You're sitting pretty. Commitments for two years. Nobody in your bracket's gambling a going motion picture career on this raw, new medium. Wait. See which way it goes."

They deserved my respect. They had it. I waited. One whole year.

During which I loved our TV "visitors," loved the *now*ness of TV itself. I even loved the commercials. The only thing I didn't love was being a spectator.

I noticed Judy, Chris and Pete were influenced by what they saw and I was, vaguely, concerned. Then, one night, after Hopalong, a new program flashed on, and before we realized what it was, we'd been treated to a real horror-picture murder closeup!

My concern was no longer vague. I was through with waiting, through with being a spectator!

Did I want to be myself? Yes. Did I believe in myself? Yes. Was I afraid to make myself responsible? No!

Well, then?

I told Tom and my agency representatives.

"When I finish this picture, I want to make no more commitments. I've simply got to go into television. It's new. It's vital and it's got to stay!"

Mr. Tom Lewis, advertising executive, producer, grinned. "Ready to be patient, dear? Takes time to build a show ..."

"Build a show! Who wants a *show*? I want to visit. I want to go into living rooms as *me*. I want ..."

"What you want, what the network wants, what will sell, and what will sell a product have to be blended."

Hmm . . .

So this wasn't going to be easy, either?

Conferences. Conferences. Conferences. Nearly two years of conferences! (I'd always thought a conference was for *deciding* something!)

Ask a monotonous question: "When do I start?" Get a monotonous answer: "Takes time, Loretta. Takes time." And all the talk, talk, talk, about format, about building a show, about finding a blend, boiled down to: only as an actress did I have any value to a network or to a sponsor. Acting—that was my ticket to go "visiting."

But, finally, I had to say: "I just can't play the same character week after week. I know at least some of my limitations. Why can't I play a different character every week?"

They bought that! Anthology, they called it.

At last, early in 1953, everyone okayed the "blend." I'd visit —as me—from my living room; introduce each story; play a different character each week; tag each story with an appropriate quotation.

I was rarin' to go. "Wait, Loretta," they said. "We have to make a pilot."

"For *what?* Who's not satisfied *now?*"

"To find out if a sponsor will buy it. The Morris Agency will show the pilot to the advertising agencies; they'll show it to prospective sponsors; they'll show it to their Brand-Executives —it'll take thirty to ninety days . . ."

Be—and Believe

My patience exploded. My patience expired!

To be available for the "visiting" I wanted, I was registered as unavailable at every major motion picture studio; had turned down every picture offered.

"Believe in yourself. Make yourself responsible."

Oh, I had, Mr. Rockett. I certainly had!

Had I been brash? Over-confident?

I asked God to help me. He did: with a renewed patience and a deepened awareness of the power of Faith *and* the right emphasis.

"Believe in yourself." Yes.

But first: "*Believe.*" Ah, yes!

We made the pilot. It was screened for its first potential sponsor, Procter and Gamble and for the first six years on television, *The Loretta Young Show* was sponsored by Procter and Gamble.

I had wanted to go "visiting."

"Like Kate Smith," I had said, because her warmth and friendliness had brought such goodness into our living-room.

Sometimes I wonder: how often do I have to learn the same thing? How could I have said such a thing? (I'm sorry, Mr. Rockett. I forgot again.)

All right, so I could only be a second-rate Kate Smith!

But, by acting in stories that prove the goodness of all kinds of people, in all kinds of places; with the understanding and talents of all those who make *The Loretta Young Show* possible, what I wanted came to be—in the way that is right for *me*.

The Things I Had to Learn

It seems to me, it's high time I thank Corinne Griffith!

Suppose she hadn't been so gorgeous, so first-rate? Suppose I'd never copied her? Mr. Rockett might never have noticed me at all.

Or would he?

Who cares?

She was.

I did.

He did.

CHAPTER FIVE

The Dream and the Real

I DIDN'T spend all my time, after I was six, dreaming my dreams of being rich and famous and ermine-clad. I measured out time enough to dream the dreams all little girls dream sooner or later.

These dreams are part and parcel of being a girl-child. I believe they're the "voice" of the woman each girl-child will someday be; the way the child and the woman, who will travel together for all the days of the rest of their life, meet. And, in time, come to know each other.

The child and the woman have a seeking to do. They've a

finding to make sure of, and, I believe, it is only possible to start this search in dreams.

In my dreams, I could be a Princess, and that's what I was. Like most little girls, I believed nothing less than a Prince could make my dreams come true.

While dreaming my dreams, like all little girls, I learned that a Prince is addicted to the employment of many, and very imaginative disguises. This is the Prince's way of being sure that the Princess will love him for himself alone.

Of course, because he is a Prince, he can be whatever he wills. He can be a crotchety old man. Or a beggar. Or a cruel and evil tyrant. He can be a toad, even!

Too sadly when they're awake little girls often try to prove what they learn in their dreams. And even when they are no longer little girls.

At least, I like to think it is for some such enchanted reason that so many of us make the mistake of "falling in love" with the most unlikely prospects for a marriage partner; the mistake of being in such an unstoppable great hurry to make our little-girl dreams come true that we don't give the woman in us a chance to guide us very much—if at all.

I was forever "falling in love" at first sight, and being disillusioned almost before I could blink.

I was as impatient about finding my dream-man as I was about everything else I wanted.

"Tall, dark and handsome" was my teenage specification. But, remembering the dream-Prince's proclivity for disguise, I managed to get some pretty violent crushes on quite a few boys who weren't *disguised* as anything. They weren't anything!

It's a good thing for me that most of those I draped with the royal habiliments of my dream-Prince couldn't see me for dust!

By the time I was nineteen, I was still dreaming my little girl dreams. But I was not so sure I was going to find my Prince. By the time I was twenty-five, so far as I was concerned, I was *not* going to find him. Within that half-dozen years I did love someone very much and I had to learn the lesson of self-denial. The man I loved could not love me.

Within the framework of this lesson there are many others. A little girl becomes a woman if she embraces all of them, and when she does come to the end of that lesson, she has learned a great deal. She knows she can wrestle with temptation and triumph over it. She knows she can face fact—and accept it. She knows that the conventions are good things. She knows that self-respect is not a gift. It must be earned. She knows that respect for God's laws, and those which men have made, are twin bulwarks.

All the things she knows build to the fact; she *can* survive. And, surviving, thank God for the lesson—and for the blessings which come with learning it.

.

I was about twenty when a friend really gave me something to think about.

We were having one of those girl-to-girl gabfests and it was my turn to declaim. And don't think I didn't!

"The man *I* marry," I declared, "must be handsome, of course.

He must have money. He must have a wonderful sense of humor. He must be a sensational dancer, a terrific athlete. He must be absolutely, utterly devoted to me. He must have a big car . . ."

"You *are* a dreamer," my friend interrupted—quite rudely, I thought. Then, and not too kindly, "Tell me one thing, Loretta. Just what do *you* have to offer to such a dreamboat?"

Well! I was through declaiming, if nothing else!

It wasn't a very welcome lesson she gave me. Gave me? She'd smacked me and my ego right in the face with it!

And, between you and me, my conscience was on her side.

Why not? I'd never even given a thought to what I had to give to my dream-man. It hadn't even occurred to me to wonder whether I measured up to being the kind of wife my kind of man had a right to expect!

What were my dreams about—a marriage or a dancing contest? A partnership or a take-everything-give-nothing routine? A sharing of a lifetime or a greedy child's gobbling all the frosting on the cake?

"If you can dream but not make dreams your master . . ."

Thank you, Mr. Kipling. Thank you for that life-line.

And, for the whole, dismaying revelation of my dreamer's egoism, thank *you,* my dear, "rude" friend!

One day, a long while later, without any sirens going off, without any stars falling from the sky, without any recognition or realization, I went to Mass with the producer of a radio show I was to do.

I went because there was some sort of a challenge involved. At least, I think that's why. What do *you* think?

Radio producer Tom Lewis, my Radio agent Nat Wolff told me, had called the show's first rehearsal for eleven o'clock Sunday morning.

"Sorry, Nat," I said, "tell Mr. Lewis I go to eleven o'clock Mass on Sunday."

Nat called back.

"Tom Lewis says you can go to earlier Mass this Sunday."

"Tell Mr. Lewis, no, *not* this Sunday. I'm going to a party Saturday night and I'll be up late and I'm going to eleven o'clock Mass on Sunday."

Nat called back.

"He says he's going to a party Saturday night and he's going to eight o'clock Mass on Sunday."

What made the man think I cared what he was going to do?

"He says he'll take you to eight o'clock Mass with him."

I didn't believe he was going to eight o'clock Mass, but it was a fast way to get rid of the whole discussion. Poor Nat!

"Oh, fine," I said, and promptly dismissed the whole silly subject from my mind.

I thought my maid had lost her mind when I swam awake and discovered she had really meant to wake me up at that unearthly hour on that Sunday morning.

"It's seven-thirty and there's a man downstairs and he says he's to take you to church and I says you're asleep and he says

I'm to wake you up and I'm waking you up and you got to hurry!"

What kind of a man was this man? My maid, until this moment, had been like six dragons when it came to guarding my time for sleep!

I jumped out of bed and dressed in a mad rush-and-scramble and gulped some coffee. I hardly glanced at myself in the mirror as I put on a dab of lipstick. My mind was a blank— except for one question.

What kind of man *is* this man that my maid does his bidding? My maid? *I* was "doing his bidding," too! Had we all gone crazy?

My rushing carried me to the top of the stairs. There I really did snap a hold onto myself. I positively refused to rush down the stairs to meet this—this—*creature*!

So I started downstairs regal-slow and there, standing at the foot of the stairs, looking up and grinning the most attractive grin I ever saw in my whole life—was this man.

"Good morning, Miss Young," he said, and his eyes had a sparkle that could put a sunburst of diamonds to shame!

"I'm Tom Lewis," he said.

"So I see," I said, bedazzled. By his smile, I guess.

Tom and I had dated a few times before he went to New York on business not long before the holidays. About a week before Christmas he telephoned from New York. He asked if I had plans for New Year's Eve.

The Dream and the Real

I told him I did have plans. Myron Selznick was giving a huge party at his lodge at Lake Arrowhead and I was going with a carload of friends.

"Fine," Tom said, "I'll see you there."

I thought he was kidding, if I thought anything about it; and whatever I thought, I forgot.

The day after Christmas I decided not to go to Myron's party after all. It was a long drive to Arrowhead, the New Year's Eve traffic would be even more hazardous than the mountain road, and the long drive back after a late party guaranteed a dull and wearying end to a festive evening.

So I was sitting at home on New Year's Eve when the phone rang.

Tom Lewis was calling.

"I'm at Myron's—why aren't you here?" he wanted to know.

"I will be there!" I practically sang the promise, raced upstairs, dressed with the speed of sound, raced to the garage and drove like mad toward Lake Arrowhead!

I was almost to the Lake when I sifted through my exuberance and the first sensible thought entered my head. It came in the form of two questions.

Why was I driving up this perilous, dark, mountain road, alone, at near-midnight? Why hadn't I asked Tom to drive down for me?

I hadn't asked him because I hadn't even thought of it until this very second.

Why, I wasn't driving to Lake Arrowhead!

The Things I Had to Learn

I was driving to Tom Lewis!
That's how I found out.

No woman can really tell—sometimes she doesn't even realize
—all the things that she learns when the man of her life re-
places the Prince of her dreams.

Tom and I had set our wedding date and I was trousseauing
with delight and, let's face it, considerable extravagance.

One thing really troubled me. I have very fine, constantly
challenging hair and I had to put it up every single night—or
else. What would my husband think of the way that makes
any of us women look?

Well, my husband wasn't going to see me looking that way.
Somebody could design something!

And somebody did. Rex, bless his heart, created for my
trousseau the loveliest, most glamorous "night-turbans." I
thanked him—and paid his stunning bill—most gratefully.

We went to Mexico for our honeymoon and I wore my tur-
bans confidently.

We'd been married for a week when Tom asked with an
almost childlike curiosity, "Do you *always* wear those things on
your head at night?"

"Of course," I said. "Always."

"Did you—all your life?" There was a sort of disciplined
twinkle in his eyes.

"Well, not all of it," I answered. "But now I do."

He looked at me with the longest look.

"Do you wear them—for me?" he asked.

"Well, I certainly wouldn't be wearing them for anyone else!" I couldn't understand what this conversation was about.

"Would you, then, *not* wear them—for me?"

Now Tom was smiling, and I was glad, even though I was still bewildered.

Then Tom told me, "Dear, you're an actress. So, much of you belongs to all the people who see you. That is as it should be. You are also what is known as a glamour girl. Being glamorous, always, is a necessity of your particular profession. But, now, you are something else. You are my wife. I can think of nothing lovelier than the intimacy of seeing your hair up in pins— or curlers—or whatever you put it up with. And I love your face without any makeup at all. It's my wife's face. It's *mine*."

It was lovely, that moment of being divested of any need for the trappings of my professional self because they had no value at all to my marriage.

I've learned since that the basis of this little lesson applies to many other things and to many other couples, too.

Whether a career-wife is a secretary, or an account-executive, whether she's an employee or the boss, I believe she must at least try, as I have tried, to leave her professional personality, her professional attitudes wherever she works—to be *herself* when she is where her name is Mrs.

Helen coined a word a few years back and I'm taking it for the title of a lesson I learned when Tom and I gave our first dinner party. The word is "hostess-tension."

Do you have it? Well, I sure had it one night. It's a miser-

89

able thing to have, and, sadly enough, you don't really know what ails you when you've got it. I didn't, anyway.

We had planned our first dinner party and invited all our nearest, dearest friends. It was a very important event in my life. I'd always been a very casual hostess, as became the members of our household. With four girls, each having a large number of beaux, Mamma made hospitality seem very simple. There was always room for one more at the table, and enough food in the refrigerator for another plate. Nobody made any production out of it. And, somehow, whenever anyone of us gave a party, it was fun and nobody went hungry.

But as I faced my first dinner party as Mrs. Lewis, I reached deep into my dreams of perfection and wound up working like a dog for days before *the* date.

Now, I told myself, the casual belongs to your past. You must be the last word in perfect hostesses. Your table must be exquisitely beautiful. Your menu must be perfect. Your food must be superb. Your wines must be right for every course. Perfect temperatures, and the perfect vintage. Your guests must be perfectly seated, you must have their before-dinner drink-preferences and their favorite cigarettes. This must be an unforgettable party. A perfect party.

I rushed around in a great and harried hurry for days. On *the* day, I checked and double-checked everything: linen, china, crystal, the florist, the grocer, the butcher, the wine cellar, the bar, the cook, the waitress, the powder-room, the place-cards, the cigarette-boxes, the ashtrays, the music on the record-player. And then I started all over again!

The Dream and the Real

It was almost time to dress.

I was as scared as when I played my first big part. But nobody suspected I was scared then, so nobody'd know I was scared now. With this bit of self-comfort I rushed to check the lipsticks in the powder-room, the soap in the soap dish, the nuts on the coffee table and tore in to look at my beautiful, beautiful table again!

I thought I heard Tom call me. The reason I thought I heard him call me was that he *had* called me.

"Are you planning to change before our guests arrive—or later?" The twinkle in his eye proved only one thing to me. He simply had no conception whatsoever of my great and lone responsibility for this incomparably important occasion. He was as calm as—as—as if we were just having some old, old friends in for a bite!

I refused to be beguiled by that eye-twinkling of his. This was no time to relax. Anything could go wrong. Probably everything would!

I was dressed—just—when the doorbell rang. I didn't wait for the maid to answer it. I did. And from that moment until the party was over I had to take care of everything.

It was a pretty party and a quiet party. The guests behaved with the perfection of mannerliness which they all possessed.

At eleven-thirty Tom and I were alone.

Wasn't that awfully early for a wonderful, perfect party to belong to the past?

I wandered around the very quiet room. Tom was straightening the bottles behind the bar.

I felt as though I had told a very funny story and no one had laughed at all. I couldn't stand that nothingness feeling.

"Was it a nice party, Tom?" I asked.

Tom's smile was so bright that I got a lump in my throat.

"It was a beautiful party, dear."

"Was the food all right, Tom?"

"The food was superb, dear."

"Were the wines all right, Tom?"

"The wines were superb, the vintages superb, the temperatures precisely what they should be, dear."

Well, he wasn't going to tell me what I wanted to hear. I guess he couldn't. It wasn't the most wonderful party—ever. He didn't have to tell me that!

"What was *wrong,* Tom?"

I braced myself to hear whatever it was I'd neglected to do properly.

Tom came over to me, led me to the divan and wiped that bright, phoney grin off his face. He looked me right in the eye and he let me have it.

"*You* were what was wrong with your party, Loretta."

I started to protest but thought better of it. I'd asked for it. I had it. But . . .

"You were so anxious, dear. You weren't *you.* You fussed over your guests, you didn't listen to anyone—you were a dedicated, remote little maitre de—serving but not entertaining. It's all right to go all out on plans. By all means make your details as perfect as you possibly can. But, dear, when the time comes for the party, all those things are merely the background. The party is the people. And most people love to have the hostess at the party, too.

"That's the only thing you forgot to do, dear. You forgot to come to your party."

"Is that why it was a flop?"

"That's why it was only a perfect party. It wasn't a fun party. No one enjoyed your tension. They love you too much. And, they missed you."

"I—I see. Thank you, Tom."

I was dead tired. Too tired to keep that lump down in my throat any longer. I sat perfectly still and let the tears roll down my face. They were tears of failure. They didn't roll very fast.

Tom ignored them.

He brought me a glass of champagne. He started the record player. Then he came to me, the glass in his hand held high.

"To you, Madame!"

His grin was infectious and my tears weren't very enthusiastic anyway, so I grinned and I bowed and lifted my glass. "To you, m'lord."

"This is *my* dance," Tom said.

Suddenly, we were at a party!

We danced and danced and laughed and laughed.

I never had hostess-tension again.

Not ever.

But, suppose Tom had lied to me? Suppose he'd only comforted me?

The Things I Had to Learn

Come to think of it, suppose I hadn't gone to church with that man that Sunday?

Why suppose that? I did go.

And that's how come this chapter!

CHAPTER SIX

※

For the Record

DEAR COUNTESS BISMARCK:

Exactly half my life ago, I wrote you a proper little thank-you note. But that was before I knew how much I really had to thank you for—and how often I'd thank you in my heart.

Maybe you've long since forgotten that you once invited me to spend a weekend at your house. You'd never be able to imagine how excited I was! You were Mrs. Harrison Williams, the best-dressed-woman-in-the-world, and I admired you extravagantly.

Your invitation sent me scurrying from shop to shop. To

95

be the house guest, even for a weekend, of the best-dressed-woman-in-the-world, I had to be the world's best-dressed-girl. Swiftly, eagerly, expensively, I acquired my wardrobe for that weekend. Everything had to be brand new. Everything had to be a real standout.

I shudder. I literally shudder, when I remember that accumulation. And I could die when I think of my lounging pajamas! They were standout all right—brilliant, shining emerald green satin (I can hardly believe it myself—but it's only too true), trimmed with lace and trimmed still further with yards of maribou and trimmed further yet with yards of ostrich feathers!

The weekend was sheer enchantment. Your hospitality is unforgettable. I was flattered practically speechless because you placed me beside your husband at the wonderful formal dinner party on Saturday night. I thought you were utterly charming. Now, I know you were far, far more.

I learned from your gentleness and kindness. You were a perfect example of "the first proof of culture is a tender regard for the ignorant."

It was two years after I'd been your weekend guest that I met a mutual friend in Paris. She was frank. Frank? She was blunt. There are times when surgery is necessary and her's was well timed. I wasn't really as confident about my wardrobe as I wanted everyone to think I was, and when she told me that you'd said, "She's a darling girl and the worst-dressed girl I've ever seen," I wasn't hurt. I was, well—glad I'd had sense enough to feel a lack of confidence.

For the Record

I was glad I was in Paris and could go to Mainbocher, because he was one of your favorite couturiers.

He showed me a beautiful gown in black crepe. I said "It's lovely. I'll have it in pink satin, please."

You wouldn't know how cold his eyes can be. I felt literally frosted when he said, "My dear Miss Young, if good taste permitted pink satin for this design I'd have made it in pink satin."

That really gave me the clue. I'd learned a lesson. I asked for his help and kept my mouth shut.

When I got back to the hotel I felt like a baby just learning to crawl. And what else was I in the world of fashion? I comforted myself with the reminder—we all have to crawl before we can walk. I was determined to crawl as fast as possible. There wasn't any sense in trying to salvage the wardrobe I had. It was hopeless. But, by starting from scratch (what a way to describe Mainbocher!), I started to learn.

The first time I ever made the best-dressed-woman list I wanted to send you a thank-you note. I've waited a long time to thank you in writing, Madame, but I've never postponed being grateful—as I learned what I've learned—because of you.

Bless you,
Loretta Young Lewis

Dearest Pol and Bet:
Surprised?
A thank-you note from Gretch the Wretch? That it is—and

as much of a surprise to me as to you! I swore I'd never thank you for that gruesome present!

So here I am—thanking you. Very gratefully. And in writing yet!

Have you ever guessed how far-reachingly effective your little plan to "gift" me down a notch or two really was? How much I learned from it?

I was fourteen and I know now that I was very fortunate indeed. The breaks were coming my way. I took them, every one of them, as my due—and behaved accordingly.

I might very well have won the undisputed title of Miss Obnoxious—if you, dear sisters, hadn't given me that unforgettable present.

I'd come home late. You and Mamma had waited dinner for me. I didn't walk into the dining room, I made an entrance of it and throughout dinner, regaled you all with my opinions and petty complaints, one after another. I proclaimed that I intended to have a great many studio practices remedied —no one was going to push *me* around—yakkity, yakkity, yak!

Engrossed with my own concerns, plans, gripes and convictions, I didn't notice no one else said anything. Not that you had a chance to get a word in edgewise. Not that I'd have listened, anyway.

The intensity of your attention to my every word should have warned me.

But I was deaf and blind to all but *me, myself* and *I*.

Dinner finished, I asked to be excused with exquisite graciousness. It was a benevolent little concession to good manners which must have been pretty ludicrous, after my self-absorbed monopoly of the dinner conversation.

I went up the stairs, calling out the time I'd have breakfast as though a dozen servitors were awaiting my instructions!

I came to the door of my room.

Your gift was on it.

You knew my most cherished dream was of the day when there would be a star on my door.

You had put one there.

I nearly died!

It was the mangiest, ugliest, miserablest-looking example of a star anybody ever saw. You'd crumpled up a lot of old news-papers and gicked them together with glue and you'd hung the whole awful mess on my door.

You'd never done anything mean to me all my whole life before. And this, I told myself, was the meanest thing anybody ever did to anybody!

I wanted to pretend I didn't see it, but I couldn't get away with that. You'd made it so big I *had* to see it.

I wanted to protest. How could I?

I had left the table a loud-mouthed, full-blown queen. Now, I was silent. I opened the door and tip-toed into my room. I felt as bedraggled as that star looked, and it didn't help when my conscience assured me that star was exactly the kind of star I'd earned.

I swore I'd die before I'd let you know. I swore I'd never let you know!

I faced up to that star.

I had earned it *up*.

I determined I would earn it *down,* if it took me forever.

One night, weeks later, when I came home the star was gone from my door.

You've a right to know I got a lump in my throat.

I was sure my star-less door meant you were satisfied that I had learned the star's lesson.

I've told a lot of other people about the first star I ever had on my door and why it was there. It helped my conscience to tell it on myself.

Now, dearest Pol and Bet, I tell you. None of us will ever be sure I've thanked you enough. All that your star saved me from is impossible for us to know.

But I've got a pretty good guess. Haven't you?

I'm sure grateful, kids!

I do swear it.

Love,

Me

Dear Al Rockett:

I've written this letter from my heart a hundred times. But I never wrote it out on paper or mailed it to you when you were here to receive it. I put it on paper now because I don't think you ever needed to read it, Mr. Rockett. I do know I've needed to write it.

Of course I've thanked you for a lot of things—for all the

things you made me learn. But, for one particular gentle kindness I've never thanked you at all. I was too embarrassed when I first learned its lesson. Then I let so much time wind onto the spools of my yesterdays that I thought you'd be embarrassed if I forced your attention on something you'd forgotten. It couldn't have been important enough for you to remember.

I've learned enough to know that to be thanked for being a good example is an entirely tolerable embarrassment. (I wish I could be embarrassed that way—and often.)

Now, this goes back to when I was a fourteen-year-old eager-beaver. I burst into your office, unannounced. I'd rushed past your receptionist because I had a really wonderful idea which you had to know about that very instant. "Mr. Rockett!" I commanded. "Mr. Rockett, last night I was at the premiere of *Seventh Heaven* at Cathay Circle and I've already checked the papers this morning and all the critics agree with me that Janet Gaynor and Charles Farrell are sensational and they're great big new stars this morning and I've been thinking nearly all night and they were unknowns yesterday just like I am today and I think you should find me a story like *Seventh Heaven* and let me act in it and I'll be a star overnight too and you'll be the reason the studio made a lot of money and I thought I should tell you, Mr. Rockett!"

If, by any wild chance, you do remember this instance, you know I did gulp it out just like that. Like a school kid confidently reciting: one and one are two, two and two are four, four and four are eight—on and on, as far as she could go.

My self-confidence was in your hands. You could have sabotaged it. If you had, maybe I could have patched it together again. Maybe, even, I could have patched it so well the cracks would never show. Maybe.

You didn't deal in those maybe's, Mr. Rockett. You listened. You listened very carefully. I came, breathlessly, to the end of my suggestion. When you were sure I'd finished, you said, as seriously as though Jack Warner himself had just presented an idea to you. "Thanks, Gretchen, for sharing your constructive thinking with me. Keep thinking constructively—and please let me share your ideas and opinions. I value your confidence in me. Meantime, you may be sure I'll try to find the story that will make you a star."

I thanked you. My exit from your office was made with considerably more dignity than my entrance. I hurried home. I proudly reported our conversation, verbatim, to Mamma. She, too, listened carefully. Her smile was very gentle as she said,

"What a kind man, Gretchen."

That's all, Mr. Rockett.

Because my years are no longer so few and because between that day and this I've met no greater, sweeter consideration, this thank-you note means far more than if I'd written it way back then. I didn't know that I'd learned something from you that day. I didn't know it for a long time.

Sometimes, I noticed, that almost involuntarily, I was more patient, and kinder than the actual circumstances required or warranted, to a beginner who was neither so young nor so determined as I once was. In a vague sort of way I wondered why.

I know why, Mr. Rockett. You'd given me an example.

I don't expect to match it. I'm not so wise, nor anywhere near as kind. But I hope I'll recognize the opportunity to try to be a little of each whenever it comes my way.

Gratefully—for always,

Gretchen

Dear Frank Capra:

I'm sure I didn't, ever, thank you enough (maybe, horrible as it is to think of, maybe I didn't even thank you at all!) for the priceless gift you gave me a long, long time ago. It isn't enough for me to know that I have told dozens and dozens of people what you did for me and what it meant to me; I've got to be certain I have told *you*.

When you cast me in your picture *Platinum Blonde,* I was scared. I'd been scared ever since I got my first big break in *Laugh, Clown, Laugh.*

I was fourteen years old then, and soared straight up into the air when Mr. Rockett told me the part of the tight-rope walker was mine. And I fell—without a parachute—at least once a day and every day that I worked on the picture.

Laugh, Clown, Laugh was directed by one of the top directors of that time. I knew beforehand that he was brilliant, temperamental and a harsh taskmaster, and I learned the hard way why he was called a tyrant. He shattered all the young self-confidence I had and I was terrified throughout the picture. No matter how hard I tried, he ranted and raved and once even threw a chair which fortunately missed its target and didn't hit anyone else either. He'd storm at me: "You're not an actress. You know nothing about acting—absolutely nothing."

He was right. I did have everything to learn, but—telling me in front of everybody absolutely killed me.

It was too late when, at the end of the picture, he said: "I gave you a very rough time on this picture. I know that. But I'm not interested in you. Just in your performance. You gave one."

It was too late, even though what he said taught me something important. Personal feelings should not enter into business—getting the job done is all that interests the boss. For four long years after *Laugh, Clown, Laugh,* my pride made me wear, like a sort of costume, an air of self-confidence. I couldn't bear it if anyone knew I had hardly any self-confidence at all. I had to make believe I had it—I knew I couldn't, ever, be a star without it. When I went to the studio and onto the set, I'd pray, pray, pray: "Dear Father, please, please, please help me to do everything just as the director tells me —to do exactly what he wants."

I prayed that prayer on my way to work for you.

It was so quiet on your set, as quiet as a cathedral! I wondered how anyone—the crew, the cast, anyone—knew what you wanted them to do. The crew was moving about, getting things done, but no one was yelling at them and they weren't yelling back and forth at one another. I was terrified by the quiet—all my uncertainties welled into my heart and set it pounding. Then you outlined the scene to each of the players separately. I made my ears hear. I made my brain memorize every word.

You signaled for a rehearsal and my brain obediently clicked your instructions back to me. At the end of the rehearsal you walked to where I was standing and your voice was so low no one else could hear what you said.

"What do you think of this character, Loretta?" You asked me.

"Think?"

I hastened to reassure you.

"Oh, I never *think*, Mr. Capra. I *never* think about the characters I play—I just try to do what the director says."

You gave me a look I've never forgotten. There was tenderness, understanding and—well, there was sadness in it, too. I stood very still before it. Even my heart stood still, waiting for some kind of awful thing to happen. Like being fired, maybe.

You spoke in such a gentle voice. You said, "Loretta!" A smile sort of whispered across your face. "Little Loretta, you must learn to think. Nothing in your acting is more important than what you think. Acting isn't doing just exactly what the director says! It's thinking yourself into the character you're playing. It's deciding what that character would do—and then it is doing just exactly that."

You really smiled then, and I realized you thought I could

think. You looked at me as though you expected me to think right away. You looked at me as an actress. And that is the priceless gift you gave me.

You set me free!

I felt as a bird must feel when the door of its cage is opened and it knows its wings can now lift it into the sky. I still had just as much to learn, of course. Only—you'd shown me how I could do it.

I never again went back to the cage I'd built of my terrors but I've never forgotten it. I've kept polishing your gift the very best I could.

I find I don't know how I can ever thank you enough, after all. But, somehow, I am very sure that you will understand.

May our dear Father bless you—always,

Loretta

Dear George Arliss:

A very long time ago when I was very, very young, there was a fantastic excitement at the studio. It was, I discovered, because the great George Arliss had signed with 20th Century to lend his artistry to its super-production, *The House of Rothschild*.

"So what?" I wondered.

I was still "so what?" about it, when everyone seemed to expect me to drop dead or something because I was to have the extravagant honor of playing the great Mr. Arliss' daughter in this picture.

For the Record

I'd learned a lesson from Frank Capra three years before which had so fully restored my bouncing young self-confidence that if anyone wants to say I was now possessed by the superb ego of adolescence, I'll save them the trouble. I'll say it myself. And you, Sir George, would know, better than anyone, that I'm not exaggerating!

I had not been impressed when your anticipated arrival at the studio had everyone in a tizzy; nor when you actually arrived and everyone, it seemed to me, was kowtowing like an idiot. So how could I be impressed by your approval of my being cast in your picture? The only thing that did impress me was that you, a star, had the final say on every single, solitary detail of your pictures, because, for the life of me, I couldn't see why.

You were internationally renowned. So? You were the world's greatest actor, the theatre's greatest artist. So? All I could see was that you were old!

When production preparations started, I needed all the self-discipline I had to accept as final your decisions about my wardrobe, my hair-styles, my make-up—even the length of my fingernails and my eyelashes!

In silence—and in self-defense—I figured things out in my own clever little way. I simply changed something about each costume and coiffure to suit myself—at least a little—when I actually went before the cameras. To this day, Sir George, I don't know how you managed to frustrate practically each and every one of my small strategies. But you sure did!

At that particular time, while I was not impressed by George

Arliss, I was completely impressed by my conviction that acting was pure emotion. I couldn't have cared less about that thing called technique. And here I was, envied by everyone because I was working with you, the great maestro of technique! Which only meant to me, that I had to submit to every whim of your highly technical perfectionism. The whole assignment left me just plain cold.

However, ingrained respect for the elderly, sternly rigid professional mannerliness and discipline helped me to mask the exasperation I felt. In almost every scene you consistently, painstakingly and thoroughly rehearsed every one of my carefully conceived personality-clichés out of my performance. One day, I did blurt out, "It's like living in another century." And you said, in your crisp, clipped manner of speech, "Precisely, my dear."

I think that's what they call "touché."

Anyway, I kept a firm lock on my tongue after that and bided my time. The script gave me one big emotional scene. It was *my* scene and I intended to play it *my* way. When we came to the take, I did do it my way. I played it with all the emotional abandon I possessed and I loved every second of my performance.

It's a good thing I did, because my pleasure in it ended with the director's call of "Cut," and you, Sir George, said very quietly, "No. No, my dear."

Then, even more quietly, you said: "You are out of key, my dear. Your voice is too high. You are playing the entire scene off pitch, destroying its meaning to the play."

For the Record

The *play?* Well, what about *me?*

I didn't agree with one word you'd said. But, what difference did that make? You were the boss. We did the scene again. And, as you were a man of infinite patience, we did it over again—and again and again. I was exhausted. I didn't understand one thing you were talking about through all those retakes and after what seemed like nine million of them I still thought my way was best.

But, at last, and somehow, I did whatever it was you wanted. You were satisfied. I didn't like it but I was glad of one thing —now we could all go home.

I gave you literal obedience for the rest of the picture. Why beat my head against a stone wall? There was one thing I had learned. You were, without a doubt, the stubbornest man in the whole, wide world.

When I saw the finished picture, I still didn't like what you'd made me do in my scenes. Why, I didn't stand out at all! Not once! I was just the daughter of a man named Rothschild. A real second-fiddle character to George Arliss.

As the years passed, I often told interviewers of your patience —that you were a meticulous, inflexible, perfectionist—enforcing cold, technical skill all over the place. I always had to say I still didn't know what you'd been trying to teach me.

Just a few months, ago, on a TV Late, Late Show, *The House of Rothschild* was the feature. I stayed up to see it. And was my face red!

You poor, dear, wonderful, patient man!

Your great and ageless artistry was clear as crystal on that tiny screen and, after all these years, I had to write you this late, late, late letter! I knew my conscience would niggle me with its "Better late than never" until I had done so.

You see, I had learned from you without even realizing it. My subconscious was smarter than I was. I'd been playing on key, holding my performances within the structure of the play for years and, automatically, had given myself all the credit for my progress as an actress!

I've television to thank for the opportunity to see, in my maturity, how blind I was in adolescence. It was a pretty thorough experience in: "O, wad some power the giftie gie us to see oursels as others see us!"

Teamplay, I've called it. Playing in perspective, I've called it. "On key," you called it. "Technique," you called it.

But what's in a name, Sir George?

"The *play's* the thing!"

Now, Maestro, I engrave upon the record:

I am very grateful to Sir George Arliss,

"Julie Rothschild"

Dear Marc Wolf:[1]

X number of years ago, knowing I was to present the Borg-Warner Trophy for the "500" at the Indianapolis Speedway's Memorial Day Race, I thought: I'm sure to see Marc Wolf and, at last I'll thank him. Right to his face.

---

[1] Marc J. Wolf is the President of the Y. & W. Theatres Corporation of Indianapolis which operates theaters throughout the state of Indiana.

For the Record

For what?

For a lesson you taught me way back when I was fifteen.

But, I had such a wonderful, relaxed evening in the *present* (who doesn't, at Marc and Bee Zee Wolf's home?) that, thanking you for that pleasant present evening, I again failed to deliver my thanks to you for something in the long-ago past.

On the flight to Los Angeles next day, I remembered and sighed. I'd have to write you, after all.

You see, Marc, no one postpones or evades writing a letter by hand, with more genuine relief than I. Oh, it's not a lack of manners (heaven forbid!). The awful truth is, I just can't spell. Helen patiently repeats her blithe assurances that my strictly no-talent spelling makes my scribbles to her, "collectors' items!" (Why she thinks producing collectors' items should encourage me I'll never know, and neither of us has time to explore the subject.)

"They have a sort of pixie quality," she says. "Only a pixie could write 'dining steward' as 'dining stuart.'"

But, let's face it, she's always thinking up such whimsies—like calling my long scrawny neck a "swan-like throat." Our verbal stubbornnesses on that descriptive bit went on year after year until I played Queen Nefertiti for *The Loretta Young Show*. (D'you s'pose I was really enchanted with Nefertiti's story, or with the fact that she had a longer neck than mine?)

Anyway (andforheavensake), what has all this got to do with what I haven't thanked you for? You can relax, Marc.

It has nothing to do with it. It just proves that one thing can lead to another—or shouldn't it?

About my hand-written letter writing. More of the awful truth is that I have to use a dictionary to be sure I spell everything properly—and it takes hours! I have to look up a word because I don't know how to spell it and because I don't know how to spell it I can't find it and if I can't find it how can I find out how to spell it? See? (I'm very sure I need not belabor my alibi further!)

So *now:* I was fifteen years old and back then, it was customary for studio contract players to be invited to dinner parties given by the studios for visiting exhibitors when they were in town. Which, it seemed to me, was all the time!

It seemed to me that whenever I was working on a picture, exhibitors did nothing but trek to Hollywood to visit. And any dinner party to which I was studio-bidden was always in the middle of the week and on a night before I had to be at the studio by the crack of dawn. (I still think 5:30 A.M. is the crack of dawn. It is, isn't it?) So I developed and nourished a nice big, juicy peeve about the whole continual exhibitors-visits idea. And, need I add, my peeve included the visitors.

Dancing with a lot of "elderly" men was the livin', lovin' end of fun—if anybody asked me! Not that anyone ever did. The studio just asked me to the dinner parties and I just went, wearing my prettiest dress. That, I felt, was all I could or would do about it.

It never occurred to me until years later that I'd always had the privilege of declining an invitation, so my assumption that

I had to go added plenty to my peevishness. (It's even an ugly-*looking* word, isn't it?)

At one of these strictly-from-nothin' events, one of the exhibitors—a man from Indiana—asked me to dance. Automatically I got up to dance.

You were that man from Indiana, Marc. We danced in silence. Then you stopped right in the middle of the floor. You looked at me very kindly and, satisfied that I was not wearing my prettiest expression, you said very gently:

"Wait a minute, Loretta Young. Asking a lady to dance is a courtesy. I've extended it to you. You didn't—and don't—have to pick it up. Dancing is for fun—fun for both partners. There's no other reason to dance at all. Would you prefer to sit out the rest of our dance?"

You managed to say this, honestly and unsugar-coated, with such kindness! Your warm, no-criticism quality denied me any right to offense; made it easy for me to toss my peeve away without explanation or apology.

I said, "Sit out *our* dance?"

I knew you were now satisfied with my expression because you grinned. I laughed and we went whirling through the aura of curiosity our pause in the middle of the floor had created.

Not only did I thoroughly enjoy our dance, I enjoyed the whole evening. And ever since, Marc, I'm sure I've not let my manners come out second-best in any social bout with a personal peeve.

I'm also sure you do remember how rude I was, even though

you didn't remind me we'd met before when, years later, in Minneapolis, we were introduced for the second time. You were the Chief Barker of Variety Clubs International, and I was its Guest of Honor, privileged to dedicate the huge $5,-000,000 Variety Club Heart Hospital, built by Variety Clubs of the Northwest, on the campus of the University of Minnesota.

When I reminded you that we'd met before, you said, "How gracious of you to remember, Loretta." That's all—and not surprising.

I realize, you see, the bed-rock of the gentleness of your reproof to me. Self-respect and personal dignity are the strength and stature of a man, and when he has won them he can be kind, forbearing, honest and modest. He is a gentleman.

I thank you for reminding me of my manners long ago, and for your example in behavior and human relations—then and now!

Love to Bee Zee, too!

Loretta

Josie dearest,

It's quite a spell since our friendship started—when you were seven and I was five. I knew then, know now, and knew all the time in between, that you're "special." And certainly our long, close friendship proves that's no lie!

You've sailed a lot of stormy seas with me—the stormy seas of childhood, girlhood and womanhood. And how you did it, without criticism or flattery or gratuitous advice, I'll never know!

We've shared laughter, too, and our triumphs great and small, and times of tears and humiliation. In counting my blessings I count, way at the top of the list, the sweet security of your friendship. You're like a lighthouse, Josie. Civilized, adult, a daily practitioner of your religion, which is as much a part of you as your skin!

I know you'll scoff as you read this. It'll even embarrass you. I know that, too. But, Josie, I've got to write my thankfulness for your friendship on the record. *Got to!* See?

Of course it would be real easy if I weren't talking to you, but *about* you. Well, why not? I'll pretend I'm talking to an interviewer who's just asked me, "Tell me about your closest friend. Who is your closest friend?" And, of course, this is what I'll answer:

"Josie. Josephine Saenz Wayne. She's a *wonderful* person. And beautiful! Spanish and French and born in Texas. I really think she's the most beautiful person I know, but not just because she attracts attention in any gathering. Sure, she's got a beautiful face and a terrific figure and radiates good health, vitality and *great* good humor; she's as chic as a Vogue cover, a divine dancer, as charming as Claire Booth Luce and as perfectly mannered as Queen Elizabeth (her father was Dr. José Sainte Saenz, President of Consular Corps in Los Angeles for years and years). But anyone can see all this.

"To me, there's a sort of glow about Josie and it's all that I know about her that makes her most beautiful. She's so real!

Everything about her is real: her intelligence, her rare poise, her tact and gentleness; her great tolerance, charitableness and forgiveness. She's such fun to be with! She's so honest, so objective, so generous and helpful—so unself-seeking. Her self-discipline, dependability, discretion and taste are infallible. And she's so practical, so well organized. Last but not least, she is a wonderful mother—devoted, but unsmotheringly maternal—which is something pretty rare, too.

"These are the qualities that I know are behind Josie's lovely, sparkling-eyed face. And, oh yes! You should hear her beguiling, delightful laugh. I've heard it bubble forth, reassuringly, in the midst of all the confusions we have to cope with today—the frustrating, exasperating things. But, I swear it: nothing ever seems to be *uncopeable* to Josie. Perhaps that's because she has the disposition of an angel, the patience of Job and, to top everything off, she has an extraordinary capacity for laughing at herself!"

My answer is true—every single word of it—Josie, even though I know you'd probably deny all of it, except that your name is Josephine! But I'm not asking you. I'm TELLING you!

To say I am grateful for your life-long friendship is as mild an expression as I've ever heard! For I am still an aspirant; I have yet to attain so many of the virtues you seem to have always had.

But I sure intend to keep trying!

Think I'm kidding?
Gretch

For the Record

Dearest Irene:

If I were writing this about you—instead of *to* you— I'd title it: "A Trilogy of Thanks." Why? Why, because that's what it is!

My thanks to you for three examples of behavior which you'd never suspect could be a lesson to anyone—your behavior is just "doing what comes naturally" as far as you're concerned.

Now, you can't "Oh, *come* now, Loretta!" me, with that gentle-vague, compliment-deflector skill of yours. From here, I can't hear a word you say! Smart, huh?

Lesson One: One day, I had quite a run-in with a producer over a part I didn't want to play. I was under contract. I would be suspended if I refused the part and I wasn't making all-that-much-money that I could afford to be off salary. The producer and I had gone round and round, this day. Some of his arguments did make a lot of sense and I was certainly upset—and uncertain about everything else.

There was only one thing to do and I did it.

I went to church. I sat way in the back and prayed, and thought and thought, and prayed. Should I play the part? Shouldn't I play the part? Should I give up the business? Or shouldn't I? (I don't know why I got into all of this, except that it has nothing to do with what I'll be thanking you for!)

A woman had been kneeling at the altar. She ended her prayers and started up the aisle. Self-consciously, I bowed my head and covered my face with my hands. I didn't want her

to think: "That good Loretta Young—how religious she is
—how prayerful she is."

I couldn't resist looking through my fingers. I 'saw trim
little high-heeled shoes coming nearer and couldn't resist rais-
ing my face.

I needn't have worried about what that lady would think!
She'd just left the altar. The look of prayers was on her face
and in her eyes. She was utterly without consciousness of self.

She was a big star, a fine actress, a top-box-office name. She
wasn't about to be impressed by seeing Loretta Young in
church. She wasn't about to think her presence would impress
anyone, either.

I was thoroughly ashamed of my silly self-consciousness. I
bowed my head fast.

"You're awfully quick today, Lord," I murmured.

I thought, "Someday, when I know Irene Dunne, I'll tell
her that the fastest lesson I ever learned, I learned from her!"

Lesson Two: One Sunday in 1948, you and Frank were
having brunch at our house when Dore Schary phoned. He
told me I'd been nominated for the Academy Award for
"Katie" in *The Farmer's Daughter*. I was completely dumb-
founded, then wildly elated. I let out a whoop that would
have scared a Comanche and winged back to the dining room
yelling, "I've been nominated, I've been NOMINATED!"

I pranced proudly about the room while everyone beamed
at me, and you, Irene, congratulated me, and shared my excitement so warmly that I thought: "Why, Irene couldn't be more
excited if she'd received a nomination herself!" Whereupon

memory splashed a reminder into my pride-dizzy head: "Irene's already received five nominations! She must think I'm acting like a goon. Acting like a goon? I am a goon!"

My deflation was so sudden, so total, that you *guessed*. I know you did, because, with your eyes twinkling, you rescued me. You said, "You'll be even more excited the next times, Loretta!"

Bless you, Irene, for that example of the helpfulness of being aware of the sensitivities of others.

Lesson Three: The loveliest demi-tasse set I own is a constant reminder of this lesson.

You'd just had your living room redecorated when I stopped by one day. It was lovely, but you said, "There's something missing in here and I can't seem to make up my mind what it is."

I thought of a pair of Tole lamps I had. "Have you thought about a pair of Tole lamps?" I asked. And you said: "That is just what I'd love! I've looked everywhere for a pair and there just isn't a pair to be found."

It made me very happy to offer mine to you and I made mince-meat of your resistance to "taking them away" from me. I told you they belonged in your house—I was thrilled for you to have them—I'd go right home and pack them and send them to you, "yet today!"

Well! Months later, we were dining with you and Frank and I became positively lyrical over your exquisitely beautiful, fragile demi-tasse cups and saucers. A few days later I was delightedly surprised when I opened a large gift-package from you and discovered you'd sent me your whole demi-tasse set!

I rushed to the phone. I trilled, "Irene! How in the world did you happen to remember I liked them?"

Were you the sly one—gentle, as always; but sly is what I do mean and I sure deserved much worse.

"Oh," you said (and no one can be as off-hand as Dr. Frank Griffin's wife). "It just 'happened' to be one of those special little things that sticks—you know—like when someone admires your lamps, or something."

Boing!

I was literally, figuratively, utterly numb. Sure, sure, I know —I know, there could be all sorts of excuses, alibis or what-have-you—I explored them all (not even excepting amnesia), but let's face the fact. I made a promise and I forgot it! I do thank you, gratefully, Irene, for reminding me—so charmingly.

I'll never forget that lesson. After all, there's nothing complicated about what you do with a promise. You make it. You keep it. How on earth anyone can forget a promise is beyond my comprehension! It always will be.

Love you—
Loretta

Dear Z-z-z-z Wayne:[1]

I've just faced a fact I must share with you. Fortunately, there's no statute of limitations on saying "thank you."

So, I do thank you, here and now, for a "present" you gave

---

[1] Z. Wayne Griffin produced *Key to the City*, the MGM production starring Clark Gable and Loretta Young.

me quite a few yesterdays-ago. It has been a very useful present and I've valued it importantly for so long that I'm very un-proud of my dereliction in the "thank you" department!

When we were making *Key to the City* you said you had an idea to discuss with me—about the kind of costume I was to wear in the love scenes.

You told me what it was and I told you the idea was utterly ridiculous.

Whose idea *was* it—for me to play my one and only love scene in the picture dressed, of all things, as an early-in-the-20th Century "little girl"?

I expected you to share my laughter at whoever was guilty of such nonsense.

You didn't laugh with me and I thought you were out of your mind when I realized that you didn't agree with me, either! Then I got stubborn. I knew I was right.

"This," I stated, very positively, "Is not for me. Why it's crazy—completely off-beat. For me. For the scene. For the picture."

Now, I'll confess what really irked me. I wanted to look just gorgeous in that scene—glamorous, lovely, beguiling—not funny; not cute! ("Cute" was what you'd said.) And I certainly had a great big juicy mental picture of how silly I'd look in a 1906 moppet's party-dress, with its exaggeratedly low waistline and a great big wide satin sash around my hips. I couldn't see myself playing a love scene looking like Baby Snooks! Why, people would howl!

Your expression didn't change. Your calm, reasonable tone

didn't change. You just kept on driving home your point. The costume would provide "exactly the note of charming incongruity" you wanted in the scene. "You're supposed to be on your way to a costume party—that's all. Why not just try it, at least?"

The weight of our courtesy, the power of your patience finally overwhelmed me. I agreed to "just try it" for you.

Well, you were right. Exactly right.

I've been wrong very often so that wasn't the "present" you gave me, Wayne. The important thing I learned from you, and thank you for, was—and is—the lesson you taught me: two very grown-up people, two adults in business together, can engage in a discussion to which they bring completely opposite viewpoints, and at least one of them can violently oppose the other. But airing their viewpoints can still be held to a discussion and not explode into a quarrel.

If one of them is like you.

Thank you, my friend!

Loretta

Thanks, Mamma, for approving of my table today—all done up in my very best of everything—not like that other time the whole family was here—remember?

I took you to the dinig room that time, and said, "The table looks lovely, doesn't it?" You said, "Very pretty." Then you said, "Why don't you ever use the beautiful lace tablecloth Tom's mother sent you?"

"Oh, I'm saving that. It's gorgeous! No sense wasting that on the family."

The way you looked at me!

The way that look made me feel!

Even before you said, as sharply as you ever said anything to me.

" 'Waste it'—on your family? You call it 'waste' to use your best for the ones you love best?"

Then you said, "Gretchen, go get that tablecloth, and do your table over. Always share your best with your family. If your best is ever going to be wasted, you may be sure it will be on strangers!"

I'll never forget that—not ever.

Love,
Gretch the Wretch

Dear Father Keller:

Aside from the thanks all who are Christophers owe to your special awarenesses of the machinations of those who would destroy the God-given strength of our nation, who work to divide-and-conquer us and erase the freedoms Americans casually take for granted; aside from your nearly miraculous accomplishment—establishing the Christophers without financial endowment, initiation fees or even membership dues—activating good Americans of all creeds and colors into the vital, individual, daily practices of the true brotherhood of man under the Fatherhood of God; aside from these great things done in our Father's name, personal thanks are owed to you—by me. For what you said to me a decade-plus ago, when you were a visitor to the set of *Come to the Stable.*

We were not strangers. You are a long-time friend of Tom's. You knew I'd been very disturbed about parts of the first script of *Come to the Stable.* You knew I'd felt I could trust no one else to thrash out the changes I knew should be made.

Come to the Stable was the story of two nuns. As a Catholic, I knew where the script, that is, the concept of the two Sisters, was technically wrong.

Sam Engel, the producer, and Henry Koster, the director, weren't Catholics. Obviously, I'd have to assume the responsibility of meeting with them and the writers, again and again —to outline what should be done. It was my sincere conviction that this was my duty and, as I was the star, I had certain prerogatives. I knew what they were and I used them. Not this time did I use them for what was "best for Loretta," but for what I sincerely belived was best for the picture.

I reminded myself that there are those who argue that religion—that prayer—makes us weak; lets us shift our responsibilities into God's Hands. I knew too well the full truth of "God helps him who helps himself," and that we are not rendered irresponsible by seeking His help—His guidance; that, more often than not, we're forced into far greater responsibilities by His will.

So I couldn't have been more sincere in my busyness. That no one seemed overly elated to have me so busy—for free, even —was just a little cross I'd have to bear.

I knew I was right. That was all I thought about. Except that, having seen my duty, I had not shirked it.

I was to discover that God always brings us into balance— in His own way and in His own time.

You were the instrument of His will for me.

On the set that day we visited pleasantly. It was a very quiet set. You listened to my recitation of all I'd done to make sure the picture was authentic and how staunchly I'd held to what I knew was right, and that both Mr. Engel and Mr. Koster had agreed that I was right.

When you spoke, it was of other things—your prayers and plans for the Christophers. You spoke no word of praise for me.

Then you said, "Do you realize, Loretta, that for every foot of progress you make in the direction of achieving a worth-while life, you only have to take care of one inch? And trust God to take care of the other eleven inches?"

You said, "No one should shirk that one inch. We must do all in our power to fulfill every demand within our obligations to others. Ask God to help you recognize not only what you should do, but what you should not do."

And finally, just before you left, you said, "You must not, you cannot, deprive others of their responsibilities nor of their triumphs."

After you said goodbye I sat very quietly. Of course what you said was right, but I needed time to wrestle with my curiosity as to why you had said these things to me, so earnestly, after what I'd told you.

I wasn't in the next several scenes. Thank goodness, I had

a couple of hours just to sit still and unravel the *why* of what you'd said.

You hadn't reproved me. You hadn't praised me, either! Hmm. At last I found the key. You meant:

No demand had been made upon me. No one had even asked for my opinion or advice. Why, of course not! Routine production procedure included consultation with a qualified representative of the Church for that! And I had left undone some of the things I really should have done because of my preoccupation with doing things I should not have done. I had "deprived others of their responsibilities."

Well, I'd had my lesson!

I'd sure see to it that they weren't deprived of their triumphs!

Hey, wait a minute, Loretta! *You'll* see to it that they're not deprived of their triumphs?

What you had said was right. I was quite content to tend to my "inch" after that. And I really did appreciate Sam Engel's frequent and generous expressions of his appreciation of my helpfulness and for my good ideas.

I don't always remember to practice what you said, Father Keller, but I am always grateful to you for having said it and for helping me realize how vast one-twelfth of the Lord's work really is! Certainly within its confines there are more than enough responsibilities for the eagerest of beavers—including me.

Thank you, very, very much, Father,

Loretta Lewis

❧

CHAPTER SEVEN

God Said Yes

Maybe I'm twice your age; maybe I'm half of it. Maybe my job seems all glamour compared to yours; maybe you haven't a job at all. Maybe a lot of differences exist in our lives, but regardless of age or circumstances, we share a lot of things —the things that really count.

No one is ever too old, too young, too rich, too poor, to pray.

Everything I've accomplished, everything good that ever happened to me, everything I really know, has come to me as the result of prayer.

Prayer, the infallible line of communication to all-powerful God.

Prayer is power.

We share that power, you and I.

The results of prayer prove His constant care, His awareness of every single solitary one of His children.

If you believe in prayer, if you storm heaven with your prayers, almost miraculous things can happen!

A few years ago the most urgent, demanding prayer of my life was answered with almost miraculous swiftness. I believe, with all my heart, that my son's hair's-breadth escape from death was the instantaneous, positive answer to prayer.

One day when Christopher and Pete were five and four, the boys and I were taking a walk not far from our house. Suddenly, Pete, the four-year-old, took off—swift and free as a bird! Without warning, running faster than I'd ever seen him run before, he darted ahead, across the sidewalk, across the parkway, headed straight for the road.

Racing to catch him, I screamed at Christopher to stay where he was on the sidewalk; looked frantically up and down the road—a favorite short-cut speedway for fast drivers because of its light traffic—telling myself this *had* to be one of its no-traffic times.

It wasn't.

A heavy station wagon was speeding toward the curve ahead of Pete. Sheer horror overwhelmed me.

"PETE!" My shriek had a nightmare's futility.

Pete was on the road now, still about a hundred feet away from me, churning happily along on his sturdy little legs. My heart burst with imperative prayer, the words of it wrenched from me.

"GOD! *SAVE HIM!*"

It was a command.

In that instant—that eternity—I "heard" the sound of scream-ing brakes; "felt" the agony of seeing Pete limp and crushed on the pavement.

But, as though I were watching a fast-action motion picture in which a single frame is suddenly held on the screen, I saw Pete brake himself to a full stop! He stood frozen in ar-rested motion. He was only inches short of the center of the road.

Tires whining, the station wagon rounded the turn and whooshed past Pete.

Let's face the unemotional fact. Something made Pete stop. Oblivious of everything except his brand-new adventure in exploration, he was deaf to my frenzied call. He hadn't seen the station wagon. He couldn't have seen it—he was too little to see over and beyond the parked car which hid his view of the turn in the road. Even if he'd heard the approaching car, I don't believe he knew enough to realize it was a sound that meant danger to him.

Most important, what I've told actually happened in less than a fraction of the time it's taken me to tell it. What I've told happened so fast I don't believe Pete could have stopped if he had heard me, or the car, or if he'd wanted to. I don't be-lieve four-year-old reflexes have the necessary, precise control of momentum he needed.

I do believe, with all my heart, that Pete was halted, that Pete's life was saved by prayer.

God said yes. I saw Him in action that day.

No one who saw what I saw that day could doubt the power of prayer.

Another story proves the infinite tenderness with which God says yes.

Some years ago, when Eloise and Pat O'Brien's Mavourneen was about two years old, the poor little thing was critically, pathetically ill. The doctor did everything he could. He came to the end of all he knew.

He told Pat.

"No hope?" Incredulous, Pat looked down at little Mavourneen, his eyes pools of misery.

"No hope, huh?" he murmured.

He didn't believe it.

Something brushed the misery from his eyes. He straightened his shoulders, left the nursery and walked tall and purposeful, to his room. He went in and closed the door. He knelt.

He started to say his Rosary.

He stayed there on his knees all through the afternoon. He was there on his knees, stubbornly saying his Rosary, when night came. And all through the night he was there on his knees. Patient. Praying.

In the morning, the doctor came to tell him that Mavourneen had lived to reach and pass the crisis.

There was all the hope in the world now!

Almost tenderly, the doctor lifted Pat from his knees. Pat

looked at the Rosary in his hand, his eyes as blue and clear and sparkling as the lakes of Killarney.

He looked *up.*

"Thanks!" he said.

Then he grinned as only that O'Brien can. "Eloise!" he roared. "I'm hungry!"

Pat had positive faith. He had faith in God, he had faith in prayer. He prayed. His prayer was answered.

As Pat would say, "It figures."

Anyone who believes in prayer can prove the power of it.

Whenever you ask Him to help you get whatever it is you want, you can be sure you will get it if it is right for you to have it. Simple?

Yes. It is simple.

But you've got to level. You've got to submit your will to His. You can't bluff your way through prayer. You can't try to outsmart God as though He were the other half of a business deal.

But, if you do ask His help on a business deal and He says yes, you'll find yourself smart enough to overcome any obstacles in that deal as easily as though you'd sprinkled some kind of sure-fire obstacle-remover over them.

Speaking of business: once upon a time a missionary who was a family friend came to see me. He was leaving for his newly assigned missionary territory in Utah. He needed a trailer and a projection machine unit. He'd come to me for what he needed. Specifically, five thousand dollars.

I didn't have that sort of money to give him. But I did

want to help, and said I'd do all I could to raise the money from my friends.

"No, we'll work on this together," he said. "I will pray."

First thing you know, *I* got an idea!

The week before, as a matter of practiced principle, I had turned down an offer from Lux Radio Theater. The script was fine and I wanted to do the show, but, months ago, I had discovered that somewhere in the fine print of my contract there was a dandy little clause which stipulated that I had to pay the studio 50 per cent of any radio salary I earned!

I know, I know, *I* signed the contract! Didn't I read it? Of course, I didn't read it! I looked at the places where it said how long and where it said how much and I signed it. When I found out about that 50-per-cent-of-any-radio-salary-to-the-studio clause—well!

We'd gone round and round on the subject, round and round —to right back where we started from. I wanted to do radio? Fine. Do radio. But the studio gets 50 per cent of what you get. No problem.

No problem at all. I just didn't do any radio.

Now, back to "my" idea.

I called the studio and asked William Goetz if they'd waive that 50 per cent clause for one broadcast if I endorsed my whole salary to a needy, worthy cause. I told him what it was. It was so easy I had to laugh. Bill Goetz not only waived the 50 per cent clause—he said he'd like to make a personal donation!

I took a firm hold on my elation. Lux had cast the part. The show went on in two days. They'd think I was crazy if I called them now.

So I was crazy.

I said a real fast prayer and dialed the number.

The facts are these: The part had been cast the day I turned it down and the show had been in rehearsal ever since. Before I could say thanks-for-the-information, Cornwall Jackson cut in on the line. I heard, "Your call's an act of providence! Loretta, we're in real trouble. Our star's got the flu. The doctor just told me she can't do the show. Can't you park that principle of yours just this once? It would be a godsend."

"I'll say it is, Corney! It's a godsend—with a capital 'G.' I'll explain later. Right now, you've got yourself a 'leadin' lady'!"

I did the show. The missionary got his needed five thousand plus a very welcome cushion—Bill Goetz' great big, fat check.

And wait till you hear what else!

1. The studio notified me of their voluntary cancellation of that 50 per cent clause in my contract!

2. About three weeks later, the studio approved my acceptance of a request from the May Company to have a Loretta Young Day in the store. For the right to feature a Loretta Young Dress, the May Company paid me ten thousand dollars! Nothing like that ever happened to me before—or since.

According to simple, practical arithmetic, I actually received twice as much as I gave in money plus a career in radio which was a continuing added source of professional income.

"Loaves and fishes?" I'll say!

I want to share with you a story told to me about a year ago. It's about a lovely, gentle woman who was the victim of arthritis. The woman's sweetness, courage and uncomplaining tolerance of pain made her an example of fortitude to all who knew and loved her. The finest specialists did everything they could to combat her painful affliction, but she had to use a cane, then crutches; and finally, she was confined to a wheelchair. She couldn't use her hands. She couldn't raise her arms.

Her adoring husband's fortune had but one value, one meaning, to him. It could pay for the finest specialists, for around-the-clock nurses, for whatever treatments offered the slightest hope of his wife's relief from pain, for whatever treatments held the tiniest grain of hope for a cure for her.

He remembered when amassing his fortune had meant a great many things: luxury, membership in the best clubs, social position, a position of influence in the community, a showcase residence, all the trappings and paraphernalia a brilliant, gifted, determined man works to earn and put his brand on to document his achievements.

His fortune had done, obediently, everything he'd expected it to do. Now it couldn't do what meant more to him than anything ever had before. It couldn't buy what he wanted more than he'd wanted anything in his whole life.

He was a man of conscience, a methodical man. He counted his blessings daily, realistically grateful for the fact that whatever money could buy for his wife, he had the money to buy.

On every day that she was well enough, the chauffeur carried the woman to her limousine. Then he drove very carefully and slowly, so that no dip or bump in the road would jar the car. He drove mile after mile while she window-shopped.

God Said Yes

So that she need not leave the car, a drive-in was the logical place for luncheon on her "shopping" expeditions. She favored a certain drive-in and it happened that the same little car-hop waited on her each time.

One day there was a small, inexpensive statue of Christ on the lady's luncheon tray. The little car-hop said very earnestly: "Put this on the table beside your bed. I will burn candles for you. On the ninth day from today you will have no more pain."

The woman was deeply touched by the little car-hop's thoughtfulness, and because the statue was a symbol of that thoughtfulness, she did put it on the table beside her bed.

A little over a week later she lay in bed looking at the statue and thinking, wistfully, how very nice it would be if the earnestness of the little car-hop could be rewarded. The sweet little thing had been so very confident. Her disappointment would be very great indeed. She sank lower into her pillows, her hands clasped behind her head.

Slowly, afraid to believe it was true, she realized she had lifted her arms! She had lifted her arms and placed her hands behind her head! It had been, long ago, a characteristic habit whenever she was unriddling some problem. She'd not been able to do it for years.

She let the wonder of it wash over her, holding back her excitement, exploring the fact, confirming it. Finally, exulting, she called out, "My arms are behind my head! They are! They truly are! What date is it? What date is it? Is this the ninth day I've had the little statue? Is it? *Is it?*"

It was the ninth day.

Slowly, sweetly, almost holding her breath, she permitted herself to accept another gloriously welcome fact.

She was not in pain.

She is still in a wheelchair, but she can fix her own hair and put on her make-up. She can hold a book, and she can feed herself. Pain is only a remembered something she had a lot of a long time ago.

She gave the little car-hop a gift. It was only a modest gift but it took quite a bit of persuasion to make the girl accept it.

"You were sweet and generous to me and you were suffering," she said. "I had to burn the candles. God made me do it." She was unexcited, unsurprised.

I suspect she'd be a little excited, and very much surprised if she knew that because she did what God "made" her do, a substantial, anonymous donation to her parish church, and a very, very generous, anonymous donation to the Catholic hospital in her home town, were a grateful man's way of saying, "Thank you, God."

It was the only way the rich man knew.

CHAPTER EIGHT

God Said No

Iᴛ's easy, it's fun, to feel exalting gratefulness when your prayer is obviously answered. Your heart's as light as a feather. Your head's in the clouds. You're tall enough to put your fingertip-prints on the stars!

It's *not* easy, it's *not* fun, when His answer to your prayer contradicts your expectations. Your heart is weighted with the desolation of disappointment and you whine—yes, we do whine —"I didn't get what I asked for. My prayer wasn't answered."

We are wrong.

God answers every prayer surely and perfectly, no matter how bewilderingly disguised His answer may be.

Wouldn't you think we'd try to penetrate the bewilderment, or trustfully accept whatever happens, once we've asked God's specific help? Wouldn't you think we'd at least try to hear His answer; try to see what He wants us to see, and do what He wants us to do?

I was a very wanting child. I was forever wanting something and for whatever I wanted, I prayed.

The courtesy of my prayers was beyond reproach. My polite, "If it be thy will, Father," prefaced each prayer and preceded each "Amen." Beyond their utterance, the words imposed no obligation upon me. I didn't think about them or analyze them.

I took for granted: you wanted; you prayed; you got.

Well, there came the time when I wanted and I prayed and what I got was a whole lot of nothing I wanted! I was so slow in learning the lesson of it that months went by while I endured, in shallow faith, without gratitude or recognition, one of the most generously answered prayers of my whole life.

I was sixteen-going-on-seventeen. I went to see the stage play *Berkeley Square* because it was to be director Frank Lloyd's next picture.

I loved it. I simply had to play the girl in the picture. If ever a part belonged to anyone, that one belonged to me, and that kind of prestige picture, exactly right then, would make me and my career really important!

This was *it*. No doubt about it. No doubt at all.

It is a very heady wine, that kind of no-doubt-at-all. And only the very young dare to sip it.

Caution tried to get its warning in edgewise and was airily dismissed. Obstacles in my path? So I was under contract to Warners? So Fox was going to make the picture? So what?

God would fix that! All I had to do was ask Him.

Ask Him? My explicit prayers bombarded His throne. "That part in *Berkeley Square*," I *told* Him, "belongs to me, Father." Mannerliness required it; I supplied it—"If-it-be-Thy-will."

I was chock-full of complacent conviction. I even heard the crackle of paper. After I did this part the studio would tear up my old contract and I knew some very nice new clauses they'd have to put in my new one!

I was tall in patience, waiting for the studio's instruction to report to Frank Lloyd at Fox.

Days passed. Too many days passed. How tall was my patience supposed to be? Then I remembered. "The Lord helps those who help themselves." Of course!

I called my studio's Casting Director.

"Didn't Fox call for me to play the lead in *Berkeley Square*"? No, there wasn't any call from Fox.

"Are you sure?" The man was exasperatingly sure.

"Well then, you call them," I told him. I hung up. I called right back. "Tell them I'll make a test," I said.

I was proud of me—and very proud of my humility. How was I to know that humility is never present when it is declared; that the least humble are most boastful of it? Learning that was way ahead of me.

Wrapped in self-approval, I walked on air when I was called and a time set for me to make the test. Pretty smart of me to suggest it, huh?

Of course the test was merely a concession to a studio technicality. I could afford to be tolerant about it.

From where I now see that sixteen-going-on-seventeen girl's behavior, "tolerant" is a very funny word with which to describe it. May I offer a choice of words which are apropos: Condescending? Patronizing? Brother!

After the test was made, I calmly awaited the final technicality. Five little words: "You got the part, Loretta."

I got a bombshell. Louella Parsons' column headlined: "Heather Angel signed for *Berkeley Square.*"

I didn't believe it.

I stared at those *six* words until I was cross-eyed.

"It's a mistake," I said, loud and clear. "Somebody's kidding Louella."

A tiny little voice deep inside me tinkled a message: "Nobody'd dare kid Louella."

The voice wasn't lying. So where did that leave me?

The little voice tinkled again: "Somebody's been kidding Loretta."

In my suddenly desolate world, a world drenched with my tears and befogged by my bewilderment, I didn't recognize my lesson. It stayed blurred for a long, long time.

I cried and cried. I cried good and hard and most of the time. I couldn't even think much beyond: "I asked. I did not receive."

Why? Why? WHY?

There just wasn't any answer. No rhyme, no reason, no nothing.

Sad days are long days. It seemed a lifetime later, but the calendar insisted it was only three days later, when the studio notified me I'd been set for a loan-out to MGM. It was a low-budget picture. A real nothing of a picture. A thing called *Midnight Mary*. Now I ask you!

I emerged from my dreary, benumbed betrayal, aching with humiliation and seething with rebellious petulance. Discipline gave me no quarter, so I encased my gamut of horrible emotions in icy professionalism and monosyllabic obedience.

That little tinkling voice was saying things to me again. "How can you be so mad at God?" it wanted to know.

Mad at God? Me?

Why, that would be heresy!

"Well," the little voice tinkled, "if you're not mad—prove it. Accept His will."

"I *do* accept His will! I do!" I proclaimed it.

The little voice gave me no argument, it just stopped tinkling. Its silence was challenging. I had to meet that challenge.

I prayed. With all my heart.

The words didn't matter. Maybe there weren't any real words. I'm not sure. I do know my heart was in this asking.

I asked to be given understanding of His will. I asked for strength to bear what I knew was ahead of me. It would be torture, sheer torture to hear all the wonderful reports about *Berkeley Square* while I toiled in exile—in an insignificant opus which nobody'd ever hear anything about.

I learned that disappointment and humiliation are not fatal diseases.

I learned that supplication is not, and cannot be, dictation.

I was beginning to learn how to pray!

Six months later, *Midnight Mary* was released. It was a "sleeper!" A great, big, fat money-maker. Than which there is nothing lovelier, nor more important, in all the world that is Hollywood. A kid named Loretta Young was suddenly and unexpectedly (I'll say!) a Hollywood-somebody they call a top star!

She was seventeen years old now, and the world was her oyster. With a great big pearl in it—for Loretta.

"Nothing's too good for Loretta," she caroled, cradling the joys of success in her hot little hands. She'd learned a lot. But she hadn't learned as much as she thought she had.

I was sad and without triumph when, despite Frank Lloyd's masterful direction, despite Leslie Howard's magnificent, sensitive performance, despite Heather Angel's beautiful, gentle, charming portrayal of the girl, *Berkeley Square,* an exquisite, enchanting picture, was not a big, fat money-maker. Period.

Wrong as I had been in my possessiveness of that part, I was not wrong about the utter loveliness of the picture. I saw it and I loved it and what happened to it at the box-office shamed the box-office, not the picture!

But the box-office reports are The Law in Hollywood, and there's no appeal from their sentence. The fate of *Berkeley Square* sobered me a little. It cautioned me to keep awfully busy with what I was trying to learn, to keep exploring the vast inscrutability of God's will. I vowed I'd never forget the lesson He had given me—when it finally did filter into my understanding!

"Thy will, Father." I have asked for that ever since.

But, even so, I am still trying to learn the full meaning of submission to it.

No prayer is too small to receive the full power of His will.

A few years ago, it seemed to me that I met a certain woman everywhere I went. Whenever and wherever we met, she—well, she just plain irked me. Don't ask me why. I don't know why. And I'm not at all proud of this story. Whether we met at parties, at the studio, or on the street (believe me, she was the most ever-present person in my life), she always managed to irritate me.

Exasperated, I actually prayed one evening, "Dear God, please don't let her be at the party tonight. I'd just like to enjoy myself for a change."

Childish? What else? Aren't we all?

Anyway, having so prayed, I arrived at the party in a real party-mood—relaxed and cheerful. And whom do you suppose I saw the very first one of all? It was quite a shock, I must say.

I could hardly ignore her. She was receiving with the hostess!

I got the message fast this time!

I'd better stop seeing her faults right now and I'd better start looking for something tolerable about her. Remember Sylvia?

She was smiling at me, holding out her hand. She wasn't at all as I'd always thought she was. She wasn't gushing, forcing, over-vivacious. She said: "Loretta, I want to apologize for what I've thought of you. I've always resented you, always felt you disliked me. I—I realized that I was wrong when you smiled so warmly at me just now."

I smiled at *her?* Why, I thought she smiled at me! Well, what do you know! That's the way He handled my little prayer!

I got exactly what I asked for. I certainly did "enjoy myself for a change." But I sure got it in the exact reversal of my way!

I know very well the long, long road to be traveled between aspiration and achievement—the long time of learning before knowledge is possessed—and I've spent a lot of time on the bridge called believing. It spans the space between wanting-to-understand and understanding. It's from that bridge—from believing—that I tell this story.

It was hard for me to believe it, even though I knew it was true.

I need so often to be reminded, to relearn the "sweet uses of adversity." This woman's example of magnificent humility and unquestioning faith reproaches the temptation or inclination to rail against my own trials and tribulations.

The adversity which came to her has come, in its separate heartbreaking parts, to many of us—women, I mean. I know of none who have had the complete heartbreak which came to her. I do know how far short I was of such faith-filled, unassailable trust in God's wisdom when only one part of her adversity was visited upon me.

She was the mother of an adorable, almost-five-year-old son. She and her husband had never wanted their small one to be lonely. They had prayed for another child almost from the time Johnny was born.

"Please, God, don't let Johnny be lonely."

That was their prayer.

There was rejoicing when she became pregnant. Most grateful rejoicing. Little Johnny was delighted, excited, and a gleeful little partner in all the planning and welcoming preparations.

The nursery was remodeled, repainted, refurnished and filled near-to-bursting with bright new things and toys for Johnny's playmate. There couldn't have been a happier house or happier parents or a happier little boy in all the world.

One day, in her seventh month, she felt strangely ill. Examinations revealed that the unborn baby was dead.

Within the hour of this revelation, Johnny sickened. Suddenly and terribly.

She insisted upon going to the hospital with Johnny. Her husband locked the door of the once bursting-with-happiness-house and followed the two stretchers to the waiting ambulance.

Johnny had polio. Complete, paralytic polio.

The doctor told his parents he was dying.

From her own hospital bed Johnny's mother looked up at the doctor. She seemed not to breathe for an immeasurable moment—a moment grown very long and suspended in silence. Her eyes widened to hold the tears that filled them, tears that glistened and blinded but were not permitted to fall. When she did breathe, a very deep breath, she let it free its way from her ever so slowly, until it ended in a little sigh, soft and sad and lonely.

She said, "I want every single second there is with Johnny, Doctor."

She asked, "How long can I postpone what I need to have done?"

The doctor calculated the risk. He gave her the very outside limit of her time.

"With extreme care, I believe your surgery can be postponed for—perhaps a week."

"A week! Doctor, you mean Johnny will live a whole week?"

The doctor said, "It is possible. I don't *know*. I can't promise."

He had to wipe a mist from his glasses, when she said, "Oh, God *is* good! God is *kind!*

Arrangements were made for her essential care and for her husband to stay at the hospital, too.

On the fifth day, when Johnny went to sleep, the doctor slowly and very gently did the things he had to do. Then, his voice low and compassionate, he told them, "Johnny won't wake up this time."

Johnny's mother and father were so still he thought they hadn't heard. Their hands reached toward each other's and met and locked together. They had heard.

"Thank you, dear God." Soft and slow, Johnny's mother

spoke. "Thank you, Father, for giving Johnny to us for all of the whole wonderful, wonderful time of his life. Thank you. Thank you, Father."

A great shaking came over her husband. He stood up and moved away from her and he thundered, "Stop it! Stop thanking God! Our children are dead! What are you thanking God for?"

His face crumpled like a little boy's, but the tears that came, the sobs that came, were cruel, hard, reluctant. That is how those things come to a man.

Johnny's mother, her cheeks wet from her silent tears, looked at Johnny's father and saw no fault in him.

From the infinite resources of her trusting soul, she drew the wisdom and the strength to smile—the smile a woman has only for the man she loves.

They weren't parents any more. She knew her husband needed his wife, not Johnny's mother nor a woman to mother him.

She offered her very special kind of smile, and her husband received it. He held her close and she wiped his tears and she answered his questions.

"We didn't want Johnny to be lonely, darling. That's what we prayed for. Now, neither of our children can ever be lonely. That's what I thank God for."

It was an answer, not an apology.

Her husband looked at her. His love for her placed the tenderest of smiles into his eyes. He spoke in a voice so low only God and his wife could hear.

"Shouldn't we thank Him together? I'd like to do it that way."

They did it that way.

I feel totally insignificant before the grandeur of such trust! I know I shall not match it in this life, but I can keep trying to touch the hem of it.

CHAPTER NINE

✿

I Was a Teenager
Yesterday,
and I Remember . . .

SINCE 1953 television has given me the chance to be a regular weekly visitor in millions of American homes, a pleasure and good fortune that has, since 1957, been multiplied. Via *The Loretta Young Show,* I'm a regular visitor in Canadian, Australian and South American homes, too.

Of course, it is flattering to know that I'm being welcomed into so many homes, near and far, but that's the least of what the welcome means to me and to all others concerned with The Show. These visitations are a privilege, and among the things I've learned is: privileges and responsibilities are as closely linked as Siamese twins.

We know our first objective—our first responsibility—is to entertain. But we never sacrifice our basic purpose, our principles, our standards of quality, taste, wholesomeness or timeliness to do it.

Almost simultaneously with television's entry into the Lewis' family life, its influence upon the children—teenage Judy and small-fry Chris and Pete—was crystal clear.

I knew, instinctively, that there was no stopping this infant medium of the entertainment world. It was going to be the mass-audience giant of that world—and of other worlds. Communications, education, human relations. I believed its influence could be more powerful and far reaching than that of any other single medium in the history of mankind. I wanted to place all I had learned—all that I knew and all the knowledge I would acquire—into the area of that influence, because I saw the results on Judy and Chris and Pete of the good visits of TV stars like Kate Smith, Ted Mack, Kukla, Fran and Ollie, and the effects of the haphazardly assembled "entertainment" of horror stories, crime stories, gangster stories and killings.

That was way back in 1951, and since 1953 we of The Show have placed our collective talents on the scales of public approval. Our critics haven't offended us at all. We believe that being called a "sentimental half-hour" or a "Sunday night soap-opera" are compliments! What's wrong with sentiment? Nothing, except that we could all do with a little more of it! What's wrong with "soap-opera?" Nothing, except that it's clean!

Our first story-rule is: Offer solutions, don't pose problems. And our real yardstick for every story we tell is: At least one person must learn one thing in the one half-hour (minus the sponsor's commercials' time, of course) which is our concern and responsibility.

So each of us does our job the very best way we know, with the fervent hope that we will serve to entertain our viewers and serve our purpose, too.

Those who are not our critics say that our success (all right —why be coy about it?—we are successful) is due to giving the public what it wants. I don't think it's that simple, because I'm not sure the public knows what it wants. I am sure the public knows what it does *not* want. It hasn't yet become very articulate about it, or done anything much about it. We think this puts it squarely up to those who are serving the public.

Nothing has made me happier than the welcome I've received from teenagers and pre-teenagers. Their letters and the various Awards their votes have given to The Show and to me have been heartwarming indeed.

Teenagers!

They are our tomorrow, there's no doubt about that!

I was a teenager yesterday. Because I well remember how sure I was of myself when I was in my teens I'm not critical of teenagers today. If I were in my teens today I'd probably do all the same things I did before. I'm sure I'd make all the same mistakes. And I'm sure I'd learn from them just as I did before and, as far as that is concerned, I'm sure today's teenagers are very much like yesterday's.

The Things I Had to Learn

Being "teenage" is an emotional experience not to be escaped by anyone. All of its emotionalism was part of my experience, my mother's experience and my grandmother's experience, for that matter. Our Judy experienced it, too.

Of course the circumstances that surround each generation of teenagers are not the same, even though principles, ideals, standards, are—or should be—inflexibly the same.

It's been said, and I certainly subscribe to it, "Children have more need of models than of critics." Lucky for us kids that Mamma practiced this in her understanding of each of us as we collided with our teenage trials. I'm afraid my teenage convictions provided more workouts for her tolerance than Pol's or Bet's or Georgie's. I remind myself of that whenever I'm tempted to impatience by my own teenagers' convictions.

The teen years are equally, if differingly, rough on teenagers and their parents. Suddenly our small ones are tall ones! Overnight, it seems like, they're no longer the objects of our tending, and we're no longer the objects of their unquestioning obedience. I'm sure this sudden discovery is a shock to all parents. (Where did our baby go? And where, now, is the child who replaced our baby?) I believe that certainly a part of the difficulty of communication between teenagers and parents lies in their respective bewilderments.

Both parent and erstwhile child are involuntarily caged in the "suspended" quality of the teens—that state of being no longer a child, not yet a grownup. I remember, and I'm glad I do, that I was always wishing the years away, waiting with a near-intolerable impatience to be sixteen, then to be eighteen, then just to be older, older, older! I was sure I'd be something just as soon as I got rid of those long, slow teen years!

I don't think my youthful impatience was the least bit extraordinary. I think teenage impatience is just plain human nature! I think every generation has to cope with different circumstances, different problems. But it's the world that's changed. Human nature hasn't.

So while circumstances and living habits do change, the fundamentals of character are the same now as in the beginning of recorded time. The words and deeds of ancient philosophers and of the Prophets are proof of that. We—today's teenagers and yesterday's—can gain both comfort and counsel, if we'll just pay attention to the words the ancients and the Prophets left to help us. But how many of us do? I wonder why, in our own separate generations, we always think *our* problems are special? As a child, a girl and now as a woman, I'm still having to make specific, special effort to achieve the essential of personal anonymity in the area of human nature. Doesn't everyone?

If you believe that teenagers today are a greater problem than in your day—whenever that was—the Ten Commandments document the denial of that belief. After all, the Lord did not deliver the first laws of our civilization to Moses on Mount Sinai without cause. They were needed! They always have been and always will be. Within their framework is instruction for overcoming all our difficulties, no matter how much we cherish them.

In your Bible and mine, Exodus 20:3-17, are the outlines of

self-discipline and self-government for all ages. And, come to think of it, for all nations!

There's nothing new about the problem of suddenly having your child become an individual of king-size positiveness, whose opinions, judgment and acts, no matter how controversial they may seem to parents wrestling with the sudden challenge to their accustomed authority, are incontrovertible to the teenager who's wrestling with his own strange new rebellions.

During this teen-time, this in-between-time, all human beings experience the only time of life when whatever they think they *know*. "Nothing is so firmly believed as what we least know," is certainly the quotation which applies.

I haven't forgotten that I *knew* more from thirteen to nineteen inclusive, than I ever have known since. Or ever shall know. Why, at eighteen, I knew more than *anybody!* I tried to be benevolent about it. I even thought I was. But it's certainly not that way on my record!

Not so long ago I read some of my eighteen-year-old interviews. They were in some old movie-magazines at the Van Johnsons' house. Well! I couldn't believe the positiveness with which I discoursed on every subject! But there it was, in nice black print. I had to believe it. This should happen to parents of teenagers more often. I'm glad it happened to me. It really helped me to temper my opinion about teenage "obstinacy." I'd like to prove, and I hope I do prove, that I had a lesson from those way-back-then articles, even though it gives quite an advantage to my own teenagers.

Teenage time is "tip-toe" time. Why shouldn't it be? That's an affirmative quality which we who should be grown-up by now can well afford to nourish into a constructive, lasting enthusiasm. The generations to come will benefit from the enthusiasms of today's teenagers. (As though you-all don't know that!)

My teenage memories are a blend of remembered impatience, absolute convictions, the excitement of dates and dances, thrilling enthusiasms, knowing-it-all—and utter, inconsolable misery.

I spent three years being dreamily and unrequitedly crazy about a boy who didn't, ever, even give me the time of day. Thanks to my being a know-it-all, I decided he just hadn't had the opportunity to tell me how he felt. It took weeks of concentrated devotion to his sister, but finally she did get me a date. He was to take me to a dance! He was to call for me at eight!

At seven-thirty I was ready and waiting, all dressed up in my peacock-best, plus some added adornment I'd pilfered from Pol and Bet. I sat myself down in the chair nearest the door so I'd not keep him waiting one split-second. At *eleven* he arrived with another couple. He made no tardiness-apologies, but I didn't care! Blithely ecstatic, I went along to the dance. Years later I actually blushed with embarrassment when I realized the extent of his indifference but, thanks to my teenage enthusiasm and super-colossal self-confidence, I thoroughly enjoyed my date at the time. Which is when a date should be enjoyed, isn't it? (P.S. I saw this idol of my dreams a few years ago. If ever anyone had a perfect example of the difference between teenage and post-teenage convictions! Why, in heaven's name, had I ever miseried over that one? Why?)

Remembering that I did, though, has helped me to understand some of the teenage incongruities I see today. Maybe that is why! That kind of looking into the past can be a healthy, helpful thing for parents to do. Perhaps we should all do it more often!

I think the teenagers of today do have to cope with many problems—brand-new problems, problems which were non-existent in my teens, or Mamma's, or anyone's teens before this day. And in this new-problem era the teenagers are not alone. We're all beset by tensions and pressures in our speed-shrunk world—a world of supersonic jets and electronic brains; of nuclear power and man's invasion of the stratosphere; of psychiatry and tranquilizers; of roaring freeways, faster cars; of the race to conquer the boundless frontier of outer space; of a cold, cold war.

It would be wonderful if we could know how this day—our times—will be judged and recorded by its historians! Way off in 2060, I wonder what we do today will look like in perspective, and after it's been sifted through the objectivity of time.

I think we have never needed one another more than we do today—our teenagers and we who are their parents. May God grant to each of us the pattern of partnership. For, of all that exists in this churning day, His is the unchanging, unchangeable, eternal power.

Actually, I think the potential for greatness for youth has never been more valid. There are greater opportunities for learning and greater opportunities to make use of knowledge. I just can't subscribe to the fear that the youth of today's world is "going-to-the-dogs"; that the average boy and girl of today are headed for disaster. I maintain my confidence that the vast majority of today's young people will do all right, too—when the time comes—if we all do our best to understand and encourage them now.

I do think too much emphasis, too much attention is given to teenagers—to their entertainment, to doleful analyses without solutions.

In proportion to the increase in population since we parents were teenagers, just how much greater is the percentage of juvenile delinquents? I think too much is printed about the wrong behavior of teenagers, the weak and confused ones and too little space and attention is given to the millions of young people who are facing their adult life with a sharp awareness of their future responsibilities, and are preparing themselves to shoulder them.

Not too long ago, after meeting with the representatives of thirty high school newspapers, I went home impressed, warmly reassured. It was no news to any of those thoughtful youngsters that they, in a few years, are going to run this great country of ours. They were dead serious. They *care* to keep America in its high place among all nations and they have no delusion that their task will be easy. Those teenagers made it clear to me that they think fondly, possessively and protectively of our country. I'd sure hate to be the one who tried to put anything over on those young Americans!

I know that somewhere among our young people there are tomorrow's great statesmen, great writers, great teachers, great and good leaders of labor and of the American people. They may not yet know it themselves. But I know it. Now, these respective greatnesses are still way deep inside of the youngsters who will be great; but, believe me, they're not just lying dormant there.

I don't believe that American kids are indifferent. And I think we of our generation best prove we aren't.

On *The Loretta Young Show,* we have presented many stories dealing with some of the things with which our teenagers have to cope. That these stories were appreciated by both teenagers and parents has been proved by thousands of letters. An outstanding example was our teleplay "The Accused," which dealt with the sale of obscene literature to minors. We know, now, that this is only one of the subjects of deep concern to parents, to teenagers themselves and to our legislators. We know, now, that hundreds of organizations—civic, state and national—are working constantly, and are doing something to curb this brutalizing exposure of our teenagers to a problem not of their creation. We're gratefully proud of an excerpt from the Congressional Record which was sent to us by Congressman John P. Saylor of Pennsylvania. Because his remarks go beyond praise of our effort, I quote it, here.

Obscene Literature
Extension of Remarks
of
HON. JOHN P. SAYLOR
of Pennsylvania
In The House of Representatives
Wednesday, May 27, 1959

Mr. Saylor: Mr. Speaker, a great many parents all over the country are grateful that the TV Academy chose Miss Loretta Young for one of its coveted awards this year. Her program of April 26, 1959, was an outstanding moral, social and civic contribution. It portrayed vividly an alarming criminal consequence of the sale of obscene literature on newsstands; it also demonstrated the need for community wide participation in the drive to clean up the printed material available to American youth.

The general public as well as the television industry is indebted to Miss Young for her superb performance in behalf of decency. Realizing the urgent need for exposing irresponsible news dealers, producers of that show have expertly dramatized the problem a second time. Another effective use would be to make prints of the film for use at meetings of parent-teachers organizations, veterans' groups and various civic clubs.

The story emphasized that society is to blame if news vendors flaunt the laws of decency by putting salacious literature up for sale. Every adult who has any love whatsoever for his family, his neighbor's children, his community, and his country should ponder Miss Young's observation that "We are going to pay an awful price for it" unless the situation is remedied.

Anyone who is resigned to believing that the practice cannot be stopped should become acquainted with what is taking place in my district. Individuals and organizations alike have begun to demand a cleanup of newsstands, with the result that guilty news dealers have been notified that they must cease peddling filth or be prosecuted. Distributors serving the area have agreed to stop serving obscene material, not only to stands, but to outlets throughout the district.

The same vigilance is required to halt activities of direct mail houses that violate the sanctity of homes and solicit children. Parents who find that lewd material is coming through the mail have a duty to society as well as to their own boys and girls to report the offenses to their local postmasters, and other postal authorities.

The Things I Had to Learn

Last year, Congress strengthened the law to simplify prosecution of traffickers of foul and filthy printed material. How communities may implement the law is being demonstrated in several areas of my district, and I take this opportunity to congratulate all participants for their forthright courage and duty.

"The Accused" is only one proof that the stirring of our desire, back in 1951, to use our one half-hour of TV time for good purposes has come to flower and is endorsed by our viewers, both teenagers and parents!

There's not a chance that our critics, those who've said our ideas are "corny," can disturb us. We're not idiots. We don't expect to satisfy everyone. We'd probably have to start changing vice to virtue and virtue to vice if we wanted to be sure we avoided any possible chance of being labeled "corny." Actually, I like "corn." So do lots of people. I want to be sure that we present *good* corn. And we take great care to be sure of that.

Let's face it, there are those today who seem to believe that if you're nice, you're a prude; if you don't drag-race on Sunset Boulevard, you're chicken; if you don't go up in the hills and neck, you're a square. They've made some fairly big dents on the consciousness of some teenagers with their promotion of these ideas, but I believe that the promotion of the good things —respect for law and order, respect for disciplined deportment and character-building standards—will outlast what these "they" people have to say. Besides, who are "they," anyway?

Regardless of what "they" say, for myself, I don't want to do anything that will brutalize me—or any viewer—in mind

Mr. and Mrs. Thomas H. A. Lewis on their wedding day, July 31, 1940. On many special occasions I wore the dress unaltered for sixteen years.

Mr. and Mrs. Tom Lewis
thirteen years later.

Being presented to Her Majesty Queen Elizabeth of England following the 1947 Royal Command Film Performance of *The Bishop's Wife* in London.

On the Lux Theater of the Air (radio) in which I made a record number of star performances.

Courtesy of Robert Perkins

Norbert ("Brodie") Brodine, Director of Photography of The Loretta Young Show, and I on location, November 1960.

TWO QUITE DIFFERENT CHARACTERIZATIONS
FOR THE LORETTA YOUNG SHOW

As "Big Blonde," a good-hearted girl from the wrong side of the tracks, one of the roles which won me my first Emmy in 1955.

As the Japanese wife in *The Pearl*, which won me my second Emmy.

Helen Ferguson and I just after I had received my first Emmy.

On the set of The Loretta Young Show.

During a shooting day for one of The Show's teleplays.

FOR ME,
FASHIONABLE
CLOTHES ARE
ONES THAT MOVE
WITH MY BODY

Gown by Werlé

Gown by Werlé

Gown by Irene

MY TWO ALL-TIME FAVORITE PORTRAIT
PHOTOS

and spirit. We will never slant a story-focus on depravity—unless we offer an honest, upbeat solution to the problem by the time our story is told.

I want no part of making any contribution whatsoever to the despair which eventually follows downbeat thinking. And, if I simply use whatever talents I have constructively instead of destructively, what's wrong with that? In all good conscience I can find nothing wrong—period.

Above all, when our stories are told each week, we want to prove, and hope we do prove, the strength—the goodness, really—of *people*. All concerned with *The Loretta Young Show* give their understanding as well as their top talents to the purpose of The Show, which is, and I repeat it, to entertain. Then, to offer solutions, not pose problems.

I'm glad I remember my comparatively carefree teens. I remember the fun-times we all had at home. And if I were a teenager today I know that the center of my social life would be "our house." I admit that I don't understand the teenage girls who'd rather "die" than ask any of the boys they see at school or on dates, to dinner with their family. One girl who wrote to me for advice said her parents' insistently offered hospitality was her great problem! "I can't make Mom understand that you just *don't* ask a boy to your house unless you're practically engaged. *Nobody* does!"

Well, I'm on Mom's side. I can't imagine dating a boy, meeting him only outside the home. What's a home and family for if it's not the center of one's life? The "Nobody does!" of this girl's letter was the poignant part of it, to me. I was always independent. I never wanted to follow the crowd, but I think that following the crowd is more typical of teenage behavior today than in "my day." And I do deplore it. Following the crowd seems to me an almost tragic relinquishment of one's own free will. I can understand the timidities that make a youngster seek security by being a carbon copy of someone they greatly admire. I did that myself once. When I was thirteen. But I wasn't scared into it by my contemporaries. I wasn't lost in a whole group whose aim was to look alike, dress alike and do everything alike. And, if I were a teenager today, I'd cherish my independence just as I did when I was a teenager.

So I'm a square! Well, at least I'm not a square peg in a round hole, which is pretty much all that you can expect if you're concentrating all your energies on being one of several carbon copies, whose exact number depends upon how many "dearest friends" you have in your own little isolated group.

It's the girl or the boy who isn't a carbon copy who will get real attention. It's to your far greater credit to be an individual, a leader instead of a leaner. And it's in one's teens that what you're going to be after your teens must be started. Unless, of course, you don't know what you want. But how many such "vegetables" are there?

I don't hold with parents who, having merely doled out a lot of do's and don'ts, sit back, smug of conscience, and shake their heads in bewilderment over every do or don't their teenagers forget. Rufus von Kleinschmid, Chancellor of the University of Southern California said not too long ago, "We are the victims of three generations of unspanked parents." And if we are, then certainly these parents' children are equal victims.

If, in this day, the gap between parents and teenagers is beyond establishing a real communication and understanding, I think an investment of the parents' time, attention, study, caring—whatever it takes to bridge that gap—is a must. And there's no dollar price tag on it. This is an investment beyond price. It's for our tomorrow, which our teenagers will have to handle. We'll get out of tomorrow nothing greater than we've put into it, today.

The teens are the years when grownups must start transferring their reins and we've no choice about that. The teens can be wondrous years for those who are in them—the time when they take an actual hand in their development of character in preparation for their productive adult years. The "three coins" in this fountain are mental, physical and spiritual. It is tragic if a teenager throws away the chance of a brilliant, successful tomorrow by a careless, spendthrift attitude today.

Several years ago, during World War II, on his daughter's sixteenth birthday, Otto Kruger wrote Ottilie a letter. He permitted *Cosmopolitan Magazine* to publish it. It was written during a time of war, but its message isn't dated. It can never be dated. I've Otto's permission, and Ottilie's, to quote from it.[1]

My very dear Ottilie,
So the sixteenth birthday has arrived! You have been worried for such a long time that it would never come! Well, here it is.

Sixteen! Why you and your mother put so much stress on this particular event I could never understand. Why is it so important to you? To her? Well, never mind, here it is.

Because you two have attached so much importance to it, its arrival has made me think—more than a little bit. Quite sud-

[1] Reprinted by permission of *Cosmopolitan Magazine,* May, 1943.

denly and very clearly it is important to me, too. Not for the same delightfully feminine and sometimes bewildering illogical reasons you and your mother share. But because I am your father and you, my girl-child, are no longer a baby, no longer a child, yet still not quite a woman.

Welcome or not, the realization of a new responsibility is upon me.

Are you saying, "What silly things for Dad to write, when he could say them so easily? Why should he write, anyway? I'm here at home and so is he." Are you asking? "Something special on your mind, Daddy?"

Yes, darling, something special. Something as old as creation —in human experience. And I'm getting off to a darned slow start on it, that's all. Could be, I'm even stalling a bit.

Well, now, let's see. The logs in the fireplace are burning nicely; my chair is comfortable; got plenty of paper; war news is coming over the radio. H'm.

We didn't have radios during the last fracas, in 1918. Didn't know you then. Didn't know your mother either. (I met her in '19 while I was still in uniform. She said I looked awful in it.)

What I'm getting at, Ottilie, is this war business. What it means to the boys at camp and its effect on those boys and, strange as it may seem to you, my sweet, what it can mean to you and to your lovely, laughing, eager girl friends.

I was one of the boys in camp in 1918. I was part of the crazy, splendid, wild, cut-throat youth which marked all of us in camp. In any camp.

The majority of us kids, mind you, came from good, decent families. We were "perfect young gentlemen" when we signed up. But, after those first weeks in isolation camp, behind that wire fence, with no leave or weekends off, with plenty of discipline, and the sharp, violent instructions which were designed to prepare us for war, we got tougher each day. Tough, Ottilie. Rough, Ottilie.

And, because we were strong and healthy, and *young,* we were quickly toughened. Then, finally it came. Transfer to main camp. And leave! A *whole weekend* leave!

Try to think what we looked like, darling. Uniforms anything but tailored—crazy haircuts. Rushing out of that gate. Rushing madly up that road. Wildly trying to get a ride into town, or catch a jitney-bus to the car line. Two days of freedom! Boy! Oh boy! A trip to town! To see a show. Get some good eats, raise some hell. And oh, boy, oh boy!—*to date a girl*! And, we didn't care whose girl. You couldn't name anywhere we wouldn't go. You couldn't name anything we wouldn't do. We weren't boys any longer. We were men. We owned the world, that weekend. And we didn't think beyond that weekend. Why should we? Tomorrows had no great place on our schedules for the simple, elemental reason that maybe, even a little more than maybe, we wouldn't have any tomorrows. See, honey?

Girls? Sure we got girls. Weren't we in uniform (even if your mother, when I finally met her, did say I looked awful) and full of pep, just let out of that cage? And weren't our eyes bright and our smiles reckless and, because of that very reckless quality, appealing? And weren't the girls, bless them, anxious to show us a good time? Anxious to lend their young laughter and zest for fun to our determination to laugh and have that fun? Wasn't it their patriotic duty to entertain the boys? Sure! Sure, Ottilie, to all of that! Saturday afternoon and Sunday. Such a short time. You know, dear, how short your weekends seem during school year.

So it was such a short time. Still, the things you can do! The scrapes you can get into! The girls you can meet!

Are you getting the idea, Ottilie?

Yes, our time was very short, and we were very young, sped on by the urgency of flying hours. Name anything! We were ready for it. Give us a little encouragement. Some of us didn't even need any encouragement. Try to stop us! We were full steam ahead and the brakes were off. Some of the girls were nice girls, some not so nice.

But they were *girls*!

We didn't remember just then, the girls at home. Sure we wrote them. But that was letter writing. Those girls were home. These girls were *here*.

We went back to camp. Of course, that wasn't after all, a last leave. Back to town, parties, girls, parties, girls.

Some of the fellows got pretty serious. Some became engaged. Some were married. But *all* of us said, "Darling, I love you."

Because of our youth we accepted the gamble on no tomorrows with not much fear. There wasn't much brooding about what lay ahead of us. Because of our youth only today was real. It was all that mattered. So most of us—not all, honey, I grant you—but most of us, as I say, just took advantage of "such a short time." "We may never see each other again." "We may not come back at all." "We're shipping out." "This is our last day!" "This is our last night!" "I love you!" *"Goodbye!"*

So, Ottilie, darling, that's the way it went through all those war-crazy months, with all those crazy kids and their girls. It's what went on in camps throughout the country. In Army camps, and Navy stations and Marine bases. With girls from nice homes. With girls from no homes at all. As I said before, some of the boys were serious, were really in love and their romances led to weddings.

There was sadness in *all* partings. And there were promises—brave, earnest promises to each other as the parting time came. Inevitably, after the boys had sailed away—*real* sadness came to some of the girls—*and* to their families.

The boys had their fighting job to do. Their days were filled with work, with dealing death, and dying. Promises back home fell overboard.

And so, a lot of the girls they left behind them were part of an unreal yesterday. Just as tomorrow had been nothing to count on, yesterday became nothing to remember. Once again, *today* was all that a guy could hold onto for sure.

Many of these girls, not really in love, much too young, mostly unmarried, became mothers.

Listen, my sweet sixteen-year-old brat, for this is why I'm writing you. Why I'm putting what I have to say to you "on the record."

It's happening again. *All* of it. It's happening again.

For American warriors are marching again. In much greater numbers, as the challenge to our freedom is greater. To farther flung points of battle, for this is *really* the World War.

But the problem of boy-meets-girl—soldier boy or sailor boy-meets-girl—is basically, just the same. Because, Ottilie, boys are boys and girls are girls. War brings their awareness of each other into sharper focus, that's all. That is, however, quite, quite, enough to inspire this letter. It is not just as an expression of my love for you and my desire to protect you. It is my duty to you, darling.

You were born when the last war was well over. You are the pride, the joy, of my maturity. You are the blessing of the man who in his youth was no less reckless, no more thoughtful of consequences than the boys who are being conditioned to defend our country today.

We had moonlight in those days, Ottilie. Yes, we had moonlight then. And we had soft music, too. The same moon shines now on a new war, on a new generation of healthy, ready to-die-if-need-be young fighters and on a new generation of eager, patriotic young girls. Its magic is as old as time. And the magic of attraction is as old as the moon. The urgency of young bodies set free from caution because only today, tonight is real, is part of the old, old pattern, too. War or no war, even.

You belong to a generation which has been told, in what may well be almost an excess of frankness, so much more than any generation was ever told before. I must make sure that you do not feel that the things you have been told are, of themselves, all the protection you may ever need. Yours is a very knowing generation, Ottie. That is because the post-war parents blamed a lot of the mistakes of the last war youth upon ignorance.

I'll tell you, honestly, honey, it wasn't just ignorance alone in 1918. It's 1942 and the boys have gone overseas, the first of them. And just as in 1918, Ottie, there is the tragedy of the girl who has been left behind.

You see what I mean, sweet? They, none of them, are to blame. In 1942 or 1918, or any year, it's so very human and natural. But those poor, unhappy girls had to go through with it then, and poor unhappy girls will have to go through it now. Those who don't stop to think, those who won't stop to clear their heads of moon, music and uniforms.

You know me better than to think I would expect you or the girls to be prudes or "arms-length-dumbbells." You know I think the girls should help show the boys in uniform a good time. You know how hard your mother works at the Canteen. But I must make sure you understand that these are mad times. I must make sure you realize how easy it is to catch the tempo of such times, and do mad things. Things for which, later, there can be—for girls—no social reparation.

You see, Ottilie, it is so easy to be mistaken. In the magic of moonlight, rhinestones can sparkle like diamonds. You can think the rhinestone is a diamond—in the moonlight. So you "buy" it. Then, when the moon is gone, you look at your "diamond" in the daylight, and see it's only a rhinestone, darling.

There's quite a conspiracy against a girl's intelligence in this problem. Because, darling, a girl can feel the excitement of the present, can feel the necessity for taking what today has to offer. She can feel the warmth of gratitude which we all have toward the boy who is going to fight and maybe die, to keep us a free nation. She can find that the moonlight or the music or the glamour of a uniform is irresistible. She can feel all of these things, Ottilie. It may be that you will, too, as this war goes on and you grow older.

That is why I had to write you—I just couldn't have sat down and talked to you and offered no excuse at all. Imagine me sitting there—looking at that pretty, sixteen-year-old face of yours, which only the day before yesterday was a baby's little red face with a small button for a nose, but even then was smiling—even though you'd no teeth to flash in that young smile.

No, I couldn't *say* these things. Although you are sixteen, to me you are still heartbreakingly young. Only, I know that you are not too young. You see, I was very young, back there in 1918. And I haven't forgotten that the girls were, most of them, even younger than the boys. I've forgotten the girls. I've forgotten their names. I've forgotten what they looked like. I think of that part of my youth tonight only because of you. Because by remembering it after all these years I can give you something to think about, young as you are. For you *must* have the chance to think of these things. Now they surround you. Your stupid old Dad has seen them before. He can recognize them.

Perhaps I'm a little old-fashioned now, and I don't want to change entirely. I've made an effort to keep up with you kids. I know I haven't quite. But on this subject, my sweet, I'm way ahead of you. No foolin'.

I am not at all sure that you need this letter, Ottie. You, with your wise little head.

But, awhile ago, I told you of a conspiracy against your intel-

ligence. Against that I give you one warning. And I write with
surgical bluntness. Because you are wise and your generation
is knowing, I'll tell you straight from the shoulder, that in the
conspiracy against you, you cannot be sure of your instinct,
honey. Your lovely, eager young body can, directed by instinct
only, betray you utterly.

You see, men have made laws to tame the laws of nature.
It is by those man-made laws, good and fine, that we live our
lives and take our places in society. When those laws are broken
the girl pays the penalty. One day you may be faced with the
need for judgment in the face of emotionalism. Keep your
mind clear, Ottie. Discount the war's urgency and the uniform.
Discount the music. Discount the moonlight.

Don't buy a rhinestone, Ottilie.

I've always tried to keep you from danger. So I have to tell
you now of what can happen—not just silently gamble on the
very likely assumption that it would never happen to *my*
daughter.

I'm almost through, darling. I feel like the boy next door
who got spanked when he told you there wasn't any Santa
Claus. Remember? And you said, "Why did they spank him,
Daddy, when he was telling the truth?" Because, I guess, honey,
that illusions last for such a little, tiny bit of our lives, we're
apt to feel it's a crime to cut their existence short.

That is all, my sweet, Sweet Sixteen.

Congratulations!

I love you very much.

> Your Dad.

Thank you, dear Otto, and *bless* you!

> Loretta.

❧

CHAPTER TEN

You Can Get What You Want

You can get what you want—*If . . .*

That little two-letter word can be either the sentinel that stops you cold or your magical "open, Sesame" to getting what you want; where you want to go and what you do with your life.

If . . . It's loaded! A real little time-bomb of a word!

Becoming its master can lift you to the heights you dream of, the success you aspire to. Letting it master you will get you no-where—and nothing.

Only because of all the things I had to learn do I dare speak so authoritatively about the part *If* plays in the life of each and every one of us. No one knows better than I that it's a very good thing indeed that the good Lord makes such a generous allowance for the *If*'s we choose and gives us such a wide margin-for-error. (Because we sure need it!)

Getting what you want is poles apart from wishing for it, and you can't start to lessen that distance until you understand that there's a vast difference between wanting and wishing.

Sooner or later, one way or another, either consciously or otherwise, you'll have to take the measure of your *If*-quotient. No one else can do that for you. It can save a lot of time *If* you don't postpone elementary self-examination. Why waste time by ignoring the inescapable?

It's obvious, it's elementary, that you can't start anywhere until you know where you want to go.

When you're sure you aren't just wishing for some wondrous gift; sure that you're prepared to work to earn what you want, then face the first really difficult test. (You're sure to flunk out on this one unless you are sternly honest with yourself about it.)

In wanting what you want, have you explored your personal limitations? Is what you want within them? (Remember, they will constantly decrease as you work toward your goal *If* you've selected the right one.)

If you are sure, then start to prepare yourself for your climb. You can count on the fact that you have to go all the way to your goal. It isn't going to climb down or wander around looking for you.

Getting anywhere in one's life time is spelled W-O-R-K. And that means hard work. Your dreams will never be anything but dreams unless you work hard to make them come true.

You Can Get What You Want

The inspiration and the promise that hard work can and will be rewarded is in the success stories of the men—every single one of them—who built our country.

Read about their dreams and their work. All the way from our Pilgrim Fathers to Henry Ford and Thomas Edison—to Walt Disney! They were all dreamers! Practical dreamers. And workers!

By all means "wish upon a star," but don't believe the rest of that lyric: "wishing will make it so." Not without work it won't. It's for sure that something has to be done to "make it so."

Disappointments are to be depended upon. *If* you let them have their way with you you'll accumulate a burden of frustration which will weigh you down so heavily that you might as well find yourself a nice little puddle of quicksand right now and settle down into it and oblivion—you and your problems together.

If you use disappointments as sort of mid-semester exams, for learning, you will learn that every disappointment you overcome makes you stronger—and wiser. The greatest success stories have been lived by those who had to grow strong and wise in that very way!

You have to cut the pattern for getting what you want. And, you'll also have to "cut" yourself to fit that pattern. Which is just another way of saying you'll have to exercise and continually develop self-discipline. There's no other way I've ever discovered to take care of: "Be good enough for what you want. Be strong enough to deserve what you want."

Everything worth while, everything of any value, has its price. Everything anyone has ever wanted has come neatly wrapped up in its penalties. *If* you want only the rewards of what you want, you're still in the dreaming stage. You aren't ready for the realities. That kind of wanting is just yearning, when you should be about the business of earning. After all you're not an infant reaching for a toy. Even an infant soon discovers that there are some toys beyond its reach and that crying for them avails nothing.

The chances are that you'll have to jettison a lot of the things you think you want. We can't have everything! It took a lot of growing up for me to realize this unalterable fact and to discipline myself into accepting it.

A long, long time ago I read an interview with Douglas Fairbanks, Sr. In it he said, "The worst thing that ever happened to you can be the best thing that ever happened to you—if you don't let it get the best of you."

I thought: "Well, that's about as meaningless a mumble-jumble of words as I've ever read." It certainly did not impress me then. It does now that I know what he meant.

Giving credit where credit is due is a very rewarding habit to form. Its rewards are inestimable. *If* we don't make it a habit we may forget to do it at all! That's taking things for granted— and *If* we do that . . .!

Well, don't do that, that's all!

Several years ago I was sitting in the sponsors' booth during a radio show. I turned to the writer. "I like this very much," I said. "You've done a magnificent job." He was a shy man. He just smiled.

Sometime later I received a script. There was a note clipped to its cover. "I couldn't forget what you said to me. I thought about it and I wrote this. I think you'll like it. Do with it what you want."

It was the script of "The Littlest Angel," by Charles Tazewell, and it became my most successful record for Decca and it is still paying me, and Mr. Tazewell, royalties. Every royalty check I receive is a reminder to give credit where credit is due!

Every time you give credit you won't actually get years-and-years of royalty checks! But, every time you give credit you can be sure you will get a dividend of one kind or another.

If you haven't already discovered this, *If* you haven't already made credit-giving one of your habits, start latching onto that habit right now. What are you waiting for?

It's heartbreaking to see many people who merely long for success. They're on a sort of treadmill, plodding along, getting exactly nowhere. They haven't mastered their dreams. They've let their dreams master them and what makes it so sad is that they don't know why others get where they want to go!

I don't believe you should just long for success or that you should ever strive for it alone.

I believe that by working at what you are doing, doing it the best you can each day, you do it better each day. And that's when success starts to sort of creep up on you! It comes very quietly when one is engrossed in doing one's very best. So that it won't disturb you, I guess.

Success can't be forced. When I left 20th Century-Fox to free-lance, my agent believed that getting big money was the way to establish real importance in our industry. He set my price at one hundred thousand dollars a picture!

I said: "I have to tell you that it seems to me the only way to get that kind of money is to prove I'm worth it, and until I play parts in which I can prove it I don't deserve it and I don't think anyone will pay it. But, I'm not my agent. Naturally, I'm willing to try it your way."

I did not work for nine months. I thought I'd go stark, raving mad with all that idleness-time. I said, then, "Myron, I like to work. I like to act. Money's only a part of what I get from my work. Please, Myron, please sign me for a picture—for whatever you can get." Myron was an understanding man.

He signed me, at far less than the amount he'd held out for, for *The Doctor Takes a Wife*.

The part gave me an excellent opportunity, led to other fine roles. As I deserved more money, Myron certainly saw that I got it! That's why I say that if you're preoccupied with being called successful, only part of your mind can be on doing the very job that will make you a success.

I believe these principles of getting what you want apply to every field of endeavor. Their results may be more spectacularly evident in my profession—my industry. But that's the only difference. I believe the rules will work in any business—in any job. Large, small or middlin'.

You Can Get What You Want

If you work only for a prize you can't have any present satisfaction in doing your job, no matter what your job is.

I remember when Tony Duquette designed and made one of his famous masks for me to wear at the Bal Masque, an Annual Charity Event. When he arrived with the finished mask he was excited. He said, "It's got to win First Prize for you!"

"I'm delighted with your mask, Tony," I said. "I think it's simply gorgeous. I don't care whether we win a prize or not! It is a lovely mask and we both know it is!"

Then I had to say what I believed. "Tony, you've made the prettiest mask you could and, please, enjoy that fact. Don't set your heart on winning the First Prize. If we don't win, you'll have had no pleasure from your fine work. You'll only be disappointed and believe me, Tony, your work deserves better than that!" And I repeated, "I don't care whether we win any prize. I just want to wear your lovely mask and I think I look very nice in it."

Tony looked at the mask and, for the first time, really saw its beauty. He grinned. "I've already got my prize—your liking it so much!"

Now we could all go to the party and enjoy ourselves! It was a beautiful party. I've never seen more beautiful women, more beautiful gowns or more beautiful masks. At eleven o'clock, the prize-winning masks were announced. You've guessed it, I'm sure.

"First Prize! To Loretta Young, wearing a mask created by Tony Duquette!"

See what I mean?

And, don't forget, I had to learn what I'd said to Tony. I didn't learn it overnight either. It takes time to learn these things.

Henry Ford, a great dreamer who worked to make his great dreams into great realities, once said: "I am convinced by my own experience that if there is any 'secret of success' it lies in the ability to get the other person's point of view and see things from his angle as well as from your own."

I'm not about to argue with anything Mr. Henry Ford ever said about success! I'm quite willing to concede that he proved himself to be an authority on that subject.

If you think getting what you want is some great big juicy solo accomplishment, then you're really a dreamer.

Wake up! Quick! And, your eyes wide-open, start using them to see how much you have to depend on the help of others! Start earning friends and I do mean *friends*. They don't come as a gift. And friendship can't be phonied! Start learning about what others are thinking. And start learning something from what *they* think.

You're pretty sure to make the right enemies, too, *If* you choose your friends and nurture your friendships with real care.

For a good fast start: LISTEN. Make yourself *listen* to what others are saying. I don't mean just "keep your mouth shut"— I mean pay attention! Honestly *hear* what is being said. "The less men think, the more they talk." Don't just wait until you see the lips of the speaker stop moving so that you can practically gulp yourself into the conversation with whatever you happen to be thinking! *If* you do, your ego-great words can only be jarring irrelevancies to those who really have been listening.

I know a very nice man who has made a fabulous amount of money. He's not impressed by that accomplishment, the result of a great and rare talent. What he wants is personal popularity! He's really a very shy, lonely, inarticulate man. He gives enormous sums to charity; he bought and staffed a huge house; he entertains constantly and lavishly. He's taken a course of charm lessons, too.

He wants so desperately to be charming that he's never relaxed. All of his dollars haven't bought what he wants because what he wants can't be bought. He wants social-confidence. I can't say, because of all his lesson-taking, that "no one has ever told him." But I can say that he has never learned lesson number one. He's not learned to listen.

At one of his most spectacular parties—a large out-of-doors party he gave to help a certain charity—he stood tirelessly in the receiving line, saying over and over, "Charming." He said it to each guest, looking beyond that guest to the one next in line!

A quiet little woman, whose husband was president of the charity organization which would benefit from this party, reached him. She shook his hand in both of hers and, her voice soft and warm with sincerity, she said:

"We are all so very grateful to you for your generosity—for your incomparable hospitality. I had to come today to thank you in person. I know that is what John would want me to do."

"Charming," the man said. "Where is John?"

The woman realized he couldn't have read the papers for several days.

"John was killed last week by a hit and run driver," she said.

"Charming, charming," the unlistening man said, smiling brightly. "Congratulations," he added, his eyes on the guest next in line.

The only one within ear-shot who did not gasp was the little widow. She gave him the sweetest, understanding smile! She pressed his hand again. "God bless you for all you've done for so many," she said. Then she moved on. I've always been proud of everyone in that room who, listening, heard—and took the cue the woman had given. Her swift exit was covered by their gaiety, as she'd wanted it to be.

This is a true, double-barreled example of what I mean. *If* you don't listen you don't hear. We can't all be as fortunate as this poor, dear man. The woman understood because she was emotionally mature. She cradled the man's insecurity in her tolerance.

As far as I'm concerned, this is an unparalleled protection of a non-listener. There's no reason to expect it can happen again or to anyone else. *If* you're one of those who need to be scared into really listening when others speak, this story ought to avail. *If* it doesn't I don't know what will!

Listening is more than just a very rewarding habit. After awhile you discover what a world of information you can gain from hearing what others say, and *If* you're interested, you're interesting. All the most popular people are good listeners. (You can check this fact for yourself. Any place. Any time.)

Sincerity is another, and not the least, of the how-to-get-what-you-want basics. The more sincerely you listen, the more you'll learn and you'll keep expanding your interests in the world around you. *If* you do that, I can promise you they'll waft you high as the moon! (And that's no longer just a gag-line!) You won't have to be an authority on every subject to enjoy it, to be enthusiastic. And, believe me, enthusiasm can really profit you!

If you have enthusiasm, you have a very dynamic, effective companion to travel with you on the road to your Somewhere. But enthusiasm isn't a substitute (nothing is, or can be) for learning your craft, no matter what talent or talents you have. *If* you don't do your job the very best of anyone, you can be as enthusiastic as a cheer-leader, you can listen like mad, you can be a smash at the biggest and best parties and still not get what you want.

Learning my craft as an actress is an ever-present challenge, a never-failing source of development. *If* one is serious about becoming a fine craftsman and *If* one works to that end—well, that one has already got a great big slice of the "cake!"

I think making mistakes is as inevitable as receiving disappointments. I don't believe, and I'm afraid I don't trust, those who say they never made or make a mistake. I'm sorry but I think that's a silly boast. *If* you say you never make a mistake, I'll bet you're just whistling in the dark because you're on the negative side of being a perfectionist. (I agree with the man who said, "A perfectionist is a coward who is afraid to make a mistake.") You've yet to discover how much can be learned from

181

making a good, old-fashioned, honest mistake and owning up to it. Mistakes can be constructive *If* you don't make the same ones over and over, or destructive *If* making a single mistake is synonymous with discouragement, in your book. You are the only one who can decide whether your mistake is a lesson or a loss.

Our mistakes can certainly help us to keep our perspective and to increase our tolerance of others. Rodgers and Hammerstein put it to words and music in *The King and I:* "This is a man who stumbles and falls but this is a man who tries!"

If you live in a world of mirrors—conscious only of yourself and what you want—how can you be sure of anything? *If* you don't read and listen and learn and submit yourself to the tests of the world outside yourself, how can you know what the world has to offer or what you've got to give to get what you want? How can you, even, know what you want? I offer a quotation from one far wiser than I: "No man was ever so much deceived by another as by himself."

As I am a woman and my blessings, for which I am very grateful, are a woman's blessings, I'd be a fool to challenge what the good Lord made me.

I think women should be feminine. Why not?

Femininity is a woman's greatest weapon!

As an actress I've lived most of my life in a highly competitive profession. And in it, I've competed as a woman. On a woman's terms. (I can't see why women even try to compete with the opposite sex on its terms.) I'm quite content to let the male exercise and enjoy his aggressive privileges while I exercise and enjoy the subtle (I hope) prerogatives of the female. I'm delighted to let men gain their goals in their way. And I purr like a kitten if I'm allowed to gain mine in my way!

If you are a woman, be aware of yourself as a woman. This doesn't mean to take undue advantage of the fact. I think it's as unfeminine to exploit one's womanly charms as it is to ignore them. If it is attention you want, by all proper means, try to get it. But remember it isn't how much, it's the *kind* of attention you attract that means you'll win or lose.

So, to get way back to the beginning of this whole subject!

If you know what you want, and *If* you accept all that goes with it, and *If* you prepare yourself for it by learning what you need to know, and *If* you can learn to see yourself in perspective, and *If* you work hard, and *If* you don't forget that you need to give more than just lip-service to the Lord, and *If* you thank Him—and all those who help you along the way—why, of *course,* you'll get what you want!

If you don't want everything, that is!

No one can ever deserve everything! And, no one can ever get everything!

There's no *If* about that little fact.

❧

CHAPTER ELEVEN

Budgeting Your Emotions

THE first time I became really conscious of what we'll call budgeting one's emotions was after *The Bishop's Wife,* starring Cary Grant, David Niven and me, was selected for the 1947 Annual Royal Command Film Performance in England. Tom and I were invited to go to London to be presented to the King and Queen.

Bag and baggage, trunks and boxes, we arrived in London on schedule. All the attendant attention and engagements between arrival time and The Command Performance were only "time-markers" for me. I just wanted to "meet" the Queen!

Finally it was Command Performance Night. Not only was I presented to Her Majesty, but I "got a lesson" from her.

I had kept my eyes on her throughout the entire evening

and, female that I am, had taken full stock of what she wore. I really had to drag my eyes away from her fabulous jewels, said eyes never having before—or since—gazed upon such rubies! Then I began to watch *her*.

She was everything I'd ever thought a Queen should be. I was sure there was something I could learn from watching her and, whatever it was, I didn't intend to miss it.

The King was a darling man—gentle, kindly and almost shy. He spoke to Tom as I stood before the Queen. I had to look way down to her from my high-heel-height of five feet seven.

I stood enchanted, before this little woman who is the epitome of dignity. She smiles with her eyes, and her smile is so warm, so personal that "regal" is too cold a word, in my vocabulary, for me to use in describing her.

Of course her charm was Queen-size! It was as exquisitely faceted and as fabulous as the rubies she wore. She spoke so graciously to me of the picture, of Samuel Goldwyn's taste in its production of Cary's performance, of David's—and of mine. But what really impressed me during all my watching of her that evening was that her dignity had no greater obvious ingredient than that she was completely unhurried.

I knew that the maintenance of such an unhurried, unharried calm had to be the result of precise, inflexible, self-discipline. My presentation to the Queen of England and having her speak to me so personally was a great and unforgettable honor. But even more important to me was my realization that this woman, as Britain's Queen, was allowed *no* margin for error! There was no permissible failure in the disciplines she must practice every day and in every way. I remembered the newsreels I'd seen during the war of the Queen, serene, smiling, unhurried and unharried, standing beside the King on the balcony of Buckingham Palace the day after the Palace had been bombed, to acknowledge the cheers of their subjects and to reassure them.

It was easy for me to practice and use the visible parts of the lesson I learned from watching her—to move slowly and calmly and control outbursts of speed provoked by the tensions of too-much-to-be-done and too-little-time in which to do it. That required only a physical discipline. But to practice the disciplines necessary to keep my emotions under control was a horse of another color. That was so anything but easy that I decided it was inhuman to expect it!

Something about that decision and its companion-dismissal of my efforts niggled me until I faced the fact that if one doesn't learn to control such inflammable stuff as one's emotions—well, that stuff can set the house on fire! It's much worse to spend yourself on profitless emotions than it is to spend hard-earned money on valueless trifles.

I was only a short step away from the obvious comparison: you budget your money, so why not your emotions?

The idea of putting a budget-label on my emotions intrigued me enough to give it an honest-to-goodness try. Why, I said to myself, that's what the Queen *has* to do!

So, self-challenged, I embarked on my adventure of self-conquest. That really is a never-ending war! You needn't take my word for it. Just ask Her Majesty, Queen Mother Elizabeth. Just watch her daughter, Queen Elizabeth II.

Or, just have a look at your own budget—household or whatever. I've come to the conclusion that balancing any kind of budget is a constant, relentless necessity. After wandering all around the mulberry bush, I arrive at the obvious!

I'm not ready to boast of my accomplishments in controlling my emotion-budget. Most of the examples of what I've learned are from the times I've *not* been able to control that budget. (I'm sometimes tempted to wonder if the man who paraphrased an old quotation into "Experience is the only school in which fools can learn" was talking about me!)

My experience in emotion-budgeting has been, and still is, varied and extensively repetitive. Just the same I have learned from it. Not enough—not nearly enough—not *yet*. But I intend to keep trying. To keep at least somewhere near that budget. After all I'm not the Queen of England. Neither are you. That means we're fortunate. We've a somewhat allowance; we're allowed some margin for error!

One thing I certainly did learn quickly. There's a vast difference between juggling one's dollars in an expense budget and struggling to hold to the budgeting of one's emotions. For one thing, you're through with your dollar as soon as you've spent it. It's gone, and that's the end of it. But expending an emotion inflates it. Unless you clamp the budget on it fast, *you're* what gets spent!

This first, quick learning had a twin—another "vast difference." That was the difference between my expert, trained knowledge as a dealer in emotions (that's what being an actress means, doesn't it?) and what I had to learn about dealing with my personal emotions.

As an actress, emotions are my business, my stock-in-trade.

As such, I've dealt in them nearly all my life. In my years of experience I've developed some professional skill and authority in handling the tools with which I work. I've also learned to protect the tools of my craft, the emotions I use in my work, as automatically and as carefully as any other craftsman—jeweler, watchmaker, toy-maker, tailor, barber, mechanic—protects his.

But as a person and as a woman, I discovered I was just as downright human-careless about my emotions as anyone else. Not until I got into my Queen-inspired emotion-budget did I realize how much of me—or anyone—gets spent on personal emotions!

Tears, for instance. Certainly tears are given to us to use. Like all good gifts, they should be used properly. There are times when a good old-fashioned cry is the perfect, comforting use of them. They wash away tensions and fears—even grief—and set you up as bright and sparkling clean as a dusty, rain-starved farm after a drought-breaking downpour. But crying to get what you want, or because you *don't* get what you want, is something else again! That's got to be taken off your emotion-budget. It belongs only in some personal-indulgence column. It's not a use—it's an abuse—of our gift of tears. Funny, isn't it, that spending, using your tears that way, leaves its label on you? Leaves you spent with self-pity (which is another no-place-for-it item on an emotion-budget), all red-eyed and sniffly. Uncomforted, dissatisfied, resentful and wanting even more than before you started to misuse those tears.

I *have* succeeded in relegating that kind of crying to my past. I simply couldn't afford it! Who can?

Personal tears *are* on my emotion-budget, though. Special

tears. To be used only for misting my eyes with a sweet, salty blindness when something wonderfully happifying happens. Those tears aren't subject to a budget-limit. There can't be a limitation on tears shed in joy or in gratitude. They are, in a way, part of a blessing. They validate the joy or the gratitude which inspired them.

As a matter of fact, there are several other emotions which should certainly be on the budget, and not limited. I discovered that putting them on the budget—to be spent fully— meant they could be controlled and could brighten my experience very profitably! These are the emotions to spend. They pay big dividends when spent.

One of the first times I used one of them—the determination to enjoy myself, deliberately and decisively—I was to go to Minneapolis, as the representative of the Motion-Picture Industry, to dedicate the $5,000,000 Variety Club Heart Hospital on the campus of the University of Minnesota. To make the trip, and fulfill my duties as my industry's representative, I had to clear five whole days of personal plans and appointments. Some of them meant a great deal to me personally.

I was conscious of a very definite regret, and felt it growing as I dutifully canceled each of those personal plans. But, for once, discipline protected my emotion-budget from disaster.

I decided I would really enjoy this five-day assignment. I relisted its responsibilities as opportunities: meeting new people; greater awareness of a part of my country I'd never visited before; the honor of dedicating a brand-new and unique hospital. (Members of the Variety Club of the Northwest had in five years collected $1,700,000 to erect, and had pledged themselves to maintain, this Heart Hospital for children of all lands, races, creeds and colors—on land donated by the University. This was the first joint project of the worlds of Education and Entertainment.)

I had a *wonderful* time!

I made no budget allowance for wasting time and emotion on any poison-dripping negative attitude. And, there wasn't any. I didn't try, in frustrating expenditures of emotion and energy, to shoulder the responsibility of fulfilling an optimistically over-scheduled three-day visit. I did only about half of what I could have tried to do. (What I did do kept me busy, for three days, from 8:00 A.M. until after midnight.) What I did, I did the very, very best I could. Which must have been all right because everyone was happy. And so was I!

I met people who welcomed me warmly and seemed like old friends; I shared the thrill of members of the Variety Club of the Northwest and their wives, who'd worked five years to make a reality of their dream of this hospital. And when Chief Barker Art Anderson turned to the University's President and said, "Minnesota, here's your hospital," I unabashedly spent some of my emotion-budget's permissible tears.

I stuck to my budget that time—and I hit the jackpot! I'm glad I didn't brag about it, though! Wrestling with that budget doesn't make you a champion the first time you lick it. I'll say it doesn't!

All the primary emotions have to be budgeted. Then all the fringe emotions, which seem to be infinite, and are unpredictable. What they can do to your emotion-budget is what termites can do to your house, or silverfish to your books. Moods, these fringe emotions are called. And true gremlins they are!

The exasperating thing about these nondescript, non-essential, non-productive, time-wasting invaders of your emotions is that if you let them accumulate, they finally provide you with the last straw. Can there be anything more exasperating than having a "straw" tilt your carefully tended budget into a cocked hat?

In the primary emotions class I've learned that the first and the most important item is love. That's the basis of what we can spend, and we never have to worry about spending too much of it. The more of that you spend, the more you have *to* spend. There's no limit to the call we can make upon that item. Knowing the fact of this, I wonder why we spend ourselves so lavishly on the emotions that shouldn't be on our budget at all!

Jealousy is one of those. Fortunately, in a few simple and surgical little lessons when I was in my early teens, my mother gave me some practical, disciplinary control of that debit item.

My first serious bout with jealousy—and it is a deadly emotion—came when I was fourteen, just getting started in my adult career. Janet Gaynor, tiny as she was, seemed to me to be getting to be a great big star and getting much better parts than I was. I realize now that the Green-Eyed Monster had blindfolded me. I could see only how much Janet was *getting*. I couldn't see how much she deserved, how incomparably appealing she was, or why I had to trail behind her; why *I* couldn't have parts as big as hers!

The worst thing about the blindfold this no-profit emotion

put over my eyes was that I could not see, and did not enjoy, the good things I *was* getting! Jealousy was really costing me!

I had no idea that it was showing on me, that I was in an almost constant state of petulance. Not until one night when I came home from seeing Janet in a picture and Mamma asked, "How was the picture?"

"Oh, fine," I answered.

"How was Janet?" Mamma asked.

"Fine. Fine. Oh, Janet was just fine—*fine*—FINE!" I exploded. "There's no reason at all why Janet should have had that part instead of me! I could have . . ."

Mamma'd had enough!

"That, Gretchen, is envy. GET RID OF IT! And right *now!* Of course you'll be constantly tempted by it because you're in a business of great competition. But you can't afford to envy everyone who plays a part you'd like to play. You probably think there is no one else who can play *any* part you happen to covet.

"Start right now to dwell on the good qualities, and the talents of your competitors. You'll soon see why they get fine parts.

"You'll get fine parts, too, when you are ready for them. But you won't get them until then, Gretchen, and you'll never get them if your envy of everyone else is getting in the way of your being ready for your own opportunities."

I realize, *now,* that I heard everything Mamma said; that, deep down inside, my conscience told me she was right.

But *then?* I just flounced out of the room!

Even though, soon after that, Janet Gaynor and I became

good friends, and have remained so through all these years, I still had many a losing battle with jealousy of others before I finally did win my victory over it.

From the standpoint of budgeting my emotions I was spend-thrift! I spent an extravagant, wasteful amount of *myself,* and so needlessly, on the deadliest, most non-productive of all emotions—envy and jealousy—before I got rid of them!

I realize, of course, that most of us go through a period of instinctive envy or jealousy. Usually, by the time one passes thirteen or fourteen, that instinctive period is over. But I didn't grow out of that period until envy and jealousy made me almost sick a few times! That is what made me realize I had to stop indulging myself unless I wanted those two awful destructive emotions to literally eat me alive!

The time-wasting emotions, on which most of us expend ourselves for no possible gain, aren't any secret. Wishing for the impossible is one of them. I know a girl who's made her consciousness a scratchy little nest of discontent because she has brown eyes and wishes her eyes were blue! Silly as that may seem to all the rest of us, her misery isn't just silly. She's genuinely unhappy.

That's an easy kind of emotional problem for any of us to see. Actually, a lot of our own problems aren't any more gruesome than hers, yet we don't always have control over them. The problems we cherish and cater to for ourselves are important only to us. Even the very same problem, in someone else's life, rarely impresses us as having any importance at all.

We really operate on a sort of two-standards basis—two sets

of values, to bring it to our budget-talk level. What *we* think versus what *anyone* else thinks, even when it's about the same thing! We all have to learn where the true values are. It's real hard work to discipline ourselves to see, and then to accept, the truth about them. Utopia isn't yet, and I don't think we'll live to see it, either.

Be that as it may, here and now I do know that setting up an emotion-budget is more than a step in the right direction. It's the practical way to start bringing more fact and less self-imposed fiction into one's daily life. I think it's Self-Protection Insurance! Only, we have to write, and underwrite, our own such policy and then we have to pay its premium. Not in dollars—in *practice*. Just forget to "pay" that premium, and watch your policy lapse, as all well-behaved insurance policies do. And then where are you?

I'm not the only one who's set up an emotion-budget. Every really busy person—all really successful people—actually operates on such a budget, consciously or unconsciously. The days of our present time are filled with all sorts of potential distractions. Too much attention is directed to rationalizing, self-forgiving analyses. We're almost over-loaded with time-saving, work-saving machinery. We've too much of what is supposed to make everything easier and not enough of the disciplines, the not-easy things which make one strong.

Sometimes it seems to me about the only thing left for a person to really *work* at is the control of one's own, very special emotion-budget. So far, at least, there's no electronic brain that can keep that in balance for us!

Discipline and poise are the essentials for the conservation of precious time and energy. Uncontrolled emotion is as undisciplined and needlessly destructive as starting a forest fire with a carelessly tossed match or cigarette. After all, forests can be replanted. And, in time, new trees can be grown. But there's no "replanting," no possible re-growing of a single one of our "unforgiving minutes." Undisciplined waste of them is a total and permanent loss. There's no forgivable time to spend on the things that are profitless, the emotions that undermine our vitality and leave us spent and dismal.

I don't think it's necessary to list all those saboteurs. After all, they're pretty obvious because they're all some kin, near or distant, to hate. If you are really alert to keeping yourself on your emotion-budget—and, obviously, discipline and poise require that of you—you won't have much trouble recognizing the emotions—large or small, "fringe" or primary—that try to sabotage that budget. (I tell this to myself constantly.)

In a way, it's mathematically sure that if your poise is showing, if you are unhurried and unharried, you're on your budget. If you're either hurried or harried or both, you poise is shattered. No one has to tell you when *that* happens and you have to whistle a fast S.O.S. to your discipline—*again!*

It would certainly be wonderful if staying on-budget were something we could get set and forget. Or would it?

If it were that simple we'd have no need of the budget. No need at all. This book wouldn't have this chapter, either!

P.S. No wonder I wonder: *what* if I hadn't "met" the Queen?

CHAPTER TWELVE

The Short Life of Bliss

To be welcome wherever you go, grooming is a must. It's also a badge of self-respect. If you don't respect yourself enough to discipline yourself into the well-groomed class, the loveliest gown from the world's most enchanting couturier-collection won't make you the belle of any ball.

You might as well have halitosis.

This, too, I had to learn the hard way.

I was a tall twelve-year-old. No longer a child, not yet a woman. A friend of Polly Ann's had what seemed to me the largest, dreamiest wardrobe in the whole world. One day when she came to the house, I was crying. Mamma'd said I could go to a dance with my sisters but I had "nothing, just nothing to wear." Pol's friend made my tears evaporate. She said I could wear something of hers! Anything I wanted! She took me to her house, opened her wardrobe-closet door and left me smack in the middle of wonderland!

My heart pounding, I scorned all her fragile, pastel formals and succumbed to a slinky, black, sequin-covered, irresistible temptation.

That night, breathless with delighted anticipation of my popularity, swinging my hips to insure the sparkle of Pol's confiscated high-heeled evening slippers, I knew that never was anyone so gorgeously arrayed as I!

My sisters, engrossed in achieving their own teenage glamour, paid no attention to my colossal accomplishment in that department. I didn't need their reassurances, anyway. No one had to tell me I was the femme fatale to end all femme fatales. Mamma, deeply preoccupied with some problem of her day, reminded us, firmly, as we left the house, that our curfew was "home at eleven o'clock."

I was never again to know such utterly blissful ignorance. As I swayed into the room, a lot of people smiled when they saw me, and whether I knew them or not I answered their smiles with bows of regal graciousness. I could tell that they were talking about me, too. Everything was going as I'd expected. I had planned to create a sensation. I was!

The dancing started. I stood and waited and watched Pol and Bet being cut in on—every few steps, it seemed to me. I decided their boy friends hadn't asked me to dance because they were just plain afraid to ask anyone so grand as I! So I smiled at them, winningly, to put them at their ease, but they didn't seem to see me. Whether they were blind or dumb, or both, they just kept right on cutting in on Pol and Bet.

It was a pretty monotonous exhibition. I had to admit that this really was a pretty dull collection of people and dull people can really ruin a party. I resolved right then and there that when I got as old as Pol and Bet I wouldn't have a bunch of zombies for my friends!

Right now though, I decided, I'd sit down. Anyway, Pol's slippers were murder! My feet were killing me.

I undulated to a chair. I sat down. I smiled. The duller the party got, the brighter I smiled.

I was the sparklingest, gaudiest, proudest wallflower who ever sat in solitary, wasted splendor.

Finally, my warmhearted wardrobe-provider arrived. When she saw me, so glittering and so lonely, she hurried across the room. She had the strangest, shocked expression on her face. When she got close enough she literally hissed at me! "Awful! It's all wrong! Wrong time. Wrong place. Wrong girl!"

Her eyes sharpened. She peered at me more closely. She sighed. "Good grief, baby! You forgot to wash your neck!"

Well, I'd had it.

I was just what I was: a twelve-year-old kid who wanted to cry.

God love her, she didn't laugh. But she gave me no false comfort. Sharply, simply, honestly and unforgettably she had etched the four essentials of grooming upon my consciousness.

The Things I Had to Learn

You must be properly dressed for the occasion, the time and place, for your age and personality. But first of all and most of all—you must be clean. Clean all over. Your hair must be clean, your skin must be clean, your teeth must be clean, your nails must be clean. Your hair must be combed, your nails manicured, your make-up tidy, your lip rouge fresh and smooth.

There's no trick to it. It takes no special talent. It is a habit which has to be developed. A habit your self-respect won't let you break. It's not vanity. It's self-respect and it's consideration for others which makes us form that habit. After all, others look at us more than we look at ourselves.

Who wants to be a One-Look Girl?

Remember me?

CHAPTER THIRTEEN

Serve, But Don't Be a Slave

I HAVE a full, rich respect for fashion. I love its whimsy, its humor, its charm and its rewards. I love its vagaries and its demands. I love what it does for women. I love what it does for me. But I know, with all my heart, that no woman should follow it blindly.

I wasn't born with that knowledge. Was anybody?

In fashion, as in everything else, there's no payoff for ignorance. A fashion-illiterate is as handicapped as the man who can't read. I had to learn that to be fashion-wise is as necessary as it is to know how to write your name and that you have to start, like a kid in kindergarten, by learning your ABC's.

The Things I Had to Learn

I've had extraordinary opportunities to know the facts of fashion. My work has brought me into contact with the world's finest designers. But I didn't take advantage of these opportunities until, thanks to the former Mrs. Harrison Williams, I discovered I was fashion-dumb!

I had a lot to learn.

I have learned a lot.

I found out you can learn a lot about yourself as a person, too—while you're learning how to use fashion in your life.

You can learn to be sure of yourself, as you learn how to use fashion, instead of letting fashion use you. If you serve, but are not a slave to fashion, the chances are you're an independent human being, too.

But, sometimes, a woman filled with all sorts of uncertainties in most of the areas of life and emotion, will have her only confidence and independence in her fashion-sense.

I'm sure this is a misfortune. Fashion should not be expected to serve in the stead of courage or character.

Norma Shearer, one of the most exquisitely groomed, best-dressed, feminine women in the world, once told me:

"I dress as carefully to take my dog for a walk on the beach as I do for an important party. I never know who may see me."

You may think that this doesn't apply to you, that you have no audience. No audience? No woman, whether housewife, school girl, working girl or professional woman, no woman is without an audience. Whether it's your family, your friends, your classmates, the people you work with—it's your audience. It deserves the best performance you can give!

I believe in being feminine.

That's what the good Lord made me. That's what I'll be.

So, of course, I love graceful clothes, clothes that move with my body. I love soft colors, exciting colors, warm colors and lively materials that shimmer or sparkle. I love furs, their soft, flattering, pliant and clinging luxury. I love hats. Feminine hats. I love hats that frame one's face.

I think hats are more than apparel. I think they are very often a woman's best friends. Whether they frame your face, tilt adventurously atop your head or serve as an anchor for an intriguing veil. There's nothing so reassuring to a woman, nor so beguiling to a man, as a breath of veil over glowing eyes. Worn, of course, at the right time and place and—for the right man.

Of course!

One day, not very long ago, in one of our large department stores, I saw a lovely creature—straight from the pages of Harper's Bazaar. She was trim, chic and glamorous. For the seashore, or for lounging in a cabana beside a swimming pool, her model-slim figure, her sleek coiffure and her grooming were beyond reproach. But! In the location where I saw her, her drop-shoulder, body-hugging, strapless, jersey bodice; her skintight, brilliantly vari-colored calypso pants; her flat, bare-foot sandals, and her mother-of-pearl toenail polish added up to an incredible, tasteless exposure of her personal charms which was embarrassing. Against the proper background this girl would have been the envy of every woman who saw her. Shopping in this out-of-place apparel, she was pitied by some, envied by none. Again, you see, it isn't what you wear, but where you wear it, that measures, labels and proclaims your fashion-literacy.

In the world of fashion the rules for acceptance are specific and they're clearly posted. Neither sheep nor mavericks will ever get to the head of the class. Ignorance is forgivable, un-orthodoxy is tolerated. Bad taste and expulsion are synonymous.

Of course, you have to have a certain imaginative, adven-turesome quality to get anywhere in the world of fashion, but there's always the right time, and the right place to break with tradition.

Shopping is a public appearance. For many women it is about as public appearance as they ever make. All women should be sure they aren't dressed for the back yard or the kitchen, the beach or a dinner dance, when they go to shop or to market.

We all love casual clothes. But let's not confuse "casual" with "careless" when we're in a casual mood. It's right and proper to dress casually to attend a sports event; a barbecue at the home of friends; to take the children to the beach or for a long drive on a hot day, to some shady spot where you stop for a roadside snack. You can even wear a midriff sunsuit or a bathing suit if you're taking the kids on a picnic, but no fashion-wise woman, no woman with any sense—fashion or otherwise—will make a sunsuit or a bathing suit her hot-weather-wardrobe from sunup to sundown. It's comfortable, I agree, but that's not what we're talking about. To be that comfortable isn't just being fashion-careless, it's being plain, downright careless. And lazy. A woman who's that sold on personal comfort is bound to be sloppy, too, in her personal relationships. Ten-to-one she'll wonder, someday, in shocked agony, why her husband isn't so much her lover as he once was.

You get out of fashion what you put into it. Just as you do out of life. If you want only its rewards, and reject its disciplines, you're stuck where you start. If you invest only a little, your dividends are limited. That's a mathematical fact so simple that even I can understand it.

The fashion-wise woman doesn't run herself frantic trying to keep up with the latest rage, fad or craze.

Styles come and go with the seasons; skirts are long or short or ballerina; they're full and petticoated or pencil-slim sheaths. Waistlines are high or low, or not at all; velvet's in, satin's out, or vice versa; hats are huge or infinitesimal. Shifting sands are rocks of Gibraltar compared to the consistent impermanencies of style.

But every fashion-wise, every best-dressed woman keeps some of her gowns for years. She's learned that fashion-wisdom is compounded of knowledge, taste, confidence and poise.

Some designers are so right, so classic, in their taste and

discretion that their gowns endure through season after season of pendulum-like changes in the mode.

Irene is an outstanding example of this class and two of her permanent beauties, designed for me, are outstanding examples of her artistry.

One: my wedding gown. I wore it, unaltered in any way, on innumerable special occasions for sixteen years!

Somewhere, I'd learned of the tradition that a wedding gown should not be packed away like a relic; that it should be worn. Worn until it is worn out. I thought it was a lovely tradition, and, thanks to Irene, I could follow it in a gown that was never style-dated. No lovely, fragile, cherished gown ever gave more enduring service, and it was always a happy gown as a wedding gown should be.

Its pastel, bouffant frothiness, achieved with yards and yards and yards of cobweb-fine silk net in the softest tones of water-lily pink and blue (my wedding flowers) finally began to grow weary, in the gown's seventeenth year. It was too weary to be worn to any more social functions. But, it was not yet worn out.

There was something so proud about it. Service-proud. It hung in my wardrobe like a tolerant dowager whose remembered loveliness rendered her impervious to competition with the merely young-prettiness of the second-generation-company in which she found herself.

I was rehearsing the dance for a dream sequence in one of our teleplays. Carey Cline, our costumer, had searched every-

where trying to find the perfect gown for the scene. It had
to be a dream-gown. It had to float and move as no gown had
ever moved—outside a dream.

There wasn't any dancing dress that seemed to know what
being a dream-dress was all about.

"Carey, it's got to have the lovely fragile quality of—of my
wedding gown . . ."

"I know," said Carey, wearily. "But . . ."

"Carey! No—no, I guess not."

"I guess not," Carey echoed.

"Why not?" I demanded. "It's perfect! I think it would love
it!"

And I was right.

No gown ever had more fun!

It yielded a dozen inches of the length of its yards and yards
and yards-wide skirt to our scissors, and billowed more full
and free in its new shortness—like a long-haired girl who'd just
had her first bob.

That's all we did. We "bobbed" its skirt. I moved in the steps
of the dance before the triple mirror in my dressing room.
Something was needed to complete the dream-ensemble. I
had it! A tiny, regal crown of rhinestones! As most certainly
became so noble a gown!

After two days of shooting the dream-dance scene, with the
lifts, and my being tossed from partner to partner, which the
dance routine required, there could be no doubt that my wedding gown, age sixteen and one-half years, was—in the very
best tradition, and in completed happiness—worn out.

The last dance scenes were shot the day after I was given

my first Emmy. When we'd finished shooting, I went to the dressing room where the reporters and photographers were waiting.

Carey asked me if I wanted to change for the pictures. I didn't. It seemed only fitting and proper that before I took off, for the last time, this most beautiful of all my gowns, we should have our picture taken together, my wedding gown and I, with Emmy and Oscar.

Just before the photographers snapped the pictures, one of them said, "What about that thing on your head? Mind taking it off?"

"Yes, I do, Elmer," I replied firmly. "My gown would like to be photographed with its crown *on*."

Elmer Holloway gave me one of those looks of benumbed patience which the whimsies of actresses bestow on the faces of photographers. Unless he reads it here, which isn't likely, Elmer still doesn't know what I was talking about. And I certainly can't blame him if he thinks I'm slightly—well, nuts? Maybe I am! Thank goodness.

Two: In 1940, Irene designed a black lace gown for me to wear in a picture, *He Came to Breakfast*. In 1950 Irene re-created the same design in delicate rose-beige lace, for me to wear in another picture. The *only* difference in the decade-apart gowns was the color!

The moral of these reminiscences is: don't throw your really lovely things away. If the design is simple, the line pure and the detail controlled with superb taste, it should be no surprise when you find that you can wear a gown proudly for

several years. I'm sure it will grow shabby from use before it
will go out of style.

If you love fads and fancies and the latest rather than the
best, then you'd better wear your clothes fast and clear your
closet of them at the end of each season. Fads just aren't for
lasting.

Sometimes a very current style can be so inexpensively priced
that the woman whose wardrobe budget is practically nil can
feel she is in the height of fashion. But unless she adds her own
personality touch to the garment in some way, she'll see herself
here, there, everywhere. It's no fun for a woman to feel she's
got on a kind of uniform, unless she's a sheep and too timid
or lazy or careless to want to leave the fold. In which case, of
course, she'll be happiest and most confident wearing what
everyone else is wearing.

But this woman will never savor the delights of fashion.
A person who is afraid to fly will never know the beauty of the
sky.

There are schools and studios where the courses in self-
improvement include fine instruction in the "secrets" of fashion,
and the really earnest student can enroll and learn—fast. As
a matter of fact, I'll bet that any woman who put her mind and
a little energy to it could learn in far less time than it took
me to do it. It won't wreck the family budget; it'll protect it
from the costliness of the mistakes you can make when you
haven't learned your fashion-alphabet. One of these studio-

chains I know about. The studios where The LORETTA YOUNG Way courses are presented.

Being in fashion isn't an isolated, personal experience. Regardless of how much, or how little, your personal wardrobe means to you—even if you ignore it—fashion still touches your world, one way or another. You might as well let it touch you becomingly—knowledgeably.

Didn't anyone ever tell you?

Ignorance is *no excuse!* That's the Law!

CHAPTER FOURTEEN

The Triplets for Every-woman—Beauty, Charm, Glamour

GLAMOUR is something no woman can be born with. It's not a gift at all. It's more of a concoction than anything else. A concoction requiring so many ingredients that it takes several giant-size industries to provide those ingredients. Because glamour has become the prize every woman seeks, billions of dollars are spent by multi-millions of women in their pursuit of it. Those who have it are envied. Those who have it not, covet it—some so deeply that they eagerly sacrifice their own precious individuality to keep up with the glamour parade. Yes, one way or another, glamour is really with us!

The Things I Had to Learn

I have been very thoughtful about the use of the word glamour ever since I discovered the dictionary definition—which I quote verbatim:

"Glamour (glam'er) n. Also glam'or (Scot glamour, glamer, corrupt of E gramarye, grammar) 1. Magic; a spell or charm. 2. Any association with an object or person, through which the object or person appears delusively glorified; a deceptive or enticing charm."

Well, all by itself that doesn't sound like something every woman should pursue like crazy!

I'm no traitor to glamour—not I! Not ever.

But I've become very realistic about it. About its scope, its service to its devotees and, most of all, I'm realistic about its limitations. I'm very realistic about the fact of its undeniable importance. But I do not hold with its being regarded as all, when it should be and only can be a Part.

As I am an actress, the use of glamour (as defined) is a facet of my business. It has to be.

As a woman I know glamour should be only a facet, too. It can't be a total. Glamour is only the superficial attractiveness —the attention-getter. It's never the sole attraction that serves a woman in her search for the things she really wants most of all.

Of course, despite the specifics which the production of glamour demands, it's really the *easiest* thing to acquire because of its total external quality. From that standpoint it's a very welcome "all" to those who prefer not to face up to the far greater demands of—well, of acquiring beauty and charm, for instance. Which, thank goodness, most women want, too.

The Triplets for Everywoman—Beauty, Charm, Glamour

There is no personal accomplishment in being born beautiful. But, it is a considerable accomplishment when a woman makes herself so vital, interesting and attractive that everyone thinks she *is* beautiful.

A face is like the outside of a house and most faces, like most houses, give us at least an idea of what we can expect to find *inside*. That's where beauty starts—where it grows—until the light of it glows through.

Believe it or not, it is true. One of the loveliest women I know has the most unrelieved assemblage of homely features I've ever seen. She's only about five feet tall. Her legs are short, her ankles thick; her hips are wide. She has thin, black, rebellious hair; small beady black eyes, a crooked nose, a somewhat receding chin.

No one can ever say her loveliness was a gift!

She used to have crooked teeth, but orthodontia corrected that; she used to have a twangy, nasal voice. She had to work very earnestly to correct that; it took her nearly three years to acquire the pleasantly modulated voice she has now.

How can she be lovely?

She is lovely because of what she is—inside. God love her, she's kind, unselfish, enthusiastic, appreciative, honest, trustworthy and by some development of inner serenity, she's totally undismayed by the short-changing she got from nature. She glows at you when she greets you. She praises and admires. She's a livin' doll in the departments of personal and human relations and many's the time she's brightened the day of some of the real beauties of our town. She couldn't compete with them but she has, and often, comforted them.

It's no wonder she has a husband who adores her!

Plenty of natural beauties meander through life in a shallow, glamour-weighted, superficial attractiveness, but they're no real threat to the girl or woman who isn't pretty at all, but who does have deep, warm, inner beauty.

If you don't believe me, take a good look at those about you and discover this fact for yourself.

There are no ugly ducklings. I don't care if your hair is straight and super-fine; your complexion sallow; your figure totally unlike a mannequin's; your eyes undistinguished; your mouth too large; your nose less than classic.

The place to start is to stop feeling sorry for yourself. The time to start is now—today!

Don't mope. I'll bet even Helen of Troy had to have at least a little sunshine in her disposition.

Step right up to your mirror and smile. Smile at what that mirror shows you. When you're smiling, what you see is already more attractive, even to yourself, isn't it? What's wrong with making a smile your first attractiveness-habit?

After you've got this nice, rewarding habit, you have to start making the most of—the best of—what nature has given you.

Your spine, for instance. Unless some misfortune has made it impossible, everyone can have good posture. Give your spine a chance. Don't slump when you sit down. Stand up when you get to your feet. Keep your rib cage up. Don't make your diaphragm work itself to exhaustion trying to pump oxygen into your lungs when you're slumping or standing—as round-shouldered as though you were a Mrs. Atlas holding the world on the back of your neck.

It'll help to tell yourself you are tall and proud. And, when you walk, walk tall—walk proud. Hang your shoulders on a mental coat-hanger and you'll find your spine is straight, your shoulders are back, your chin is up, your hips are in. And you can breathe!

Your hands, your eyes, your voice, your thoughts are your servants. Be sure you use their services for your beauty, your charm, your glamour. For your home, for your business, for *you*.

Hands are always conspicuous and if used carelessly, they'll always detract, never be a plus to the enhancement of personality. But if you learn to use them properly and gracefully, they'll make a genuine contribution to your authoritative loveliness. A contribution which is yours exclusively.

I know of a woman who was always called glamorous. A great stage actress, a star, she was noted for her beauty, too. Specifically, for her beautiful hands and eyes. When I saw her in person, some years ago, I was amazed to discover that she was actually a very plain woman. Her eyes weren't huge and dark, as I'd always thought. They were only average size—and blue! It was their expression that made them beautiful. The depth of their warmth made them look large and dark. Her famous hands weren't beautiful, either. They were even far from being perfectly shaped, but by her use of them she had made them dramatic. She created an illusion of slender, long-fingered hands by the art she'd perfected in her use of them! That was, I think, the "magic" of glamour in action! She had become an internationally noted beauty only because she had a beautiful expression in her eyes and used her hands beautifully!

The Things I Had to Learn

It is an art to use one's hands effectively, an acquired art. It can be learned. I don't mean: have fluttery hands. Good heavens, I mean anything but that! The woman who constantly "talks with her hands" proclaims her self-consciousness and broadcasts her inability to express her thoughts competently.

So, as the first step toward forming a good habit is to eliminate a bad habit, if you are using your hands for meaningless gestures, start to discipline your use of them, quick! Sit on them, if necessary. Keep them in movement only when they move in harmony with what you are saying. Your growing awareness of good, or bad, hand-usage will help you master the attractiveness of genuinely expressive hands. It takes practice—a lot of it —but artfully expressive hands will enhance both your conversation and personality-impact.

Why not give your hands the Mirror-Test? Stand before your mirror. Talk. Watch your hands. See what I mean?

Eyes do more than see. They talk, too, and they're real tattle-tales! They tell the truth about their possessor's health, composure, disposition and intelligence. They tell everything! It's up to us to make sure that what we give them to tell doesn't add up to self-betrayal! If we use them and don't abuse them, they'll serve us well and all the way.

I feel almost sad whenever I see a woman stare blankly into space. Staring destroys whatever natural beauty eyes possess and gives a very unattractive impression, either of indifference, preoccupation or just plain stupidity.

The size, shape or color of your eyes is of no importance. But their expression—what they tell—is of vital importance. If they are alert, alive, animated, they're attractive. And if they are also listening eyes, they'll tell the world you're a magnetic personality! Simple? It really is simple. You simply have to do what must be done.

There's nothing new in saying "eyes are mirrors." The poets have made it sort of a classic compliment. I don't. I'm too literal. I know that mirrors can't camouflage. What they show may not be a compliment at all! Eyes themselves are helpless. They've got to mirror what's behind them. You can only look as intelligent as you are. So, as far as I can see, eye-beauty insurance is obtainable only by one's mental development. That development is a must—a continuing, progressive one.

Of course, eye-strain is a nice, big, fat enemy of eye-beauty and it should be eliminated under the professional guidance of your optician, as should all actual eye ailments or weaknesses.

Just because you want to be glamorous, don't be a sheep about your eye make-up. Remember that make-up is to enhance, and that's all it's supposed to do! If you think that copy-catting just any make-up you see will make you model-lovely, think instead, about one thing. Remember that the lovely models who gaze from the covers or pages of Vogue and Harpers Bazaar, their gorgeous orbs often sharply, unnaturally outlined, are immobilized on those covers or pages. Don't, please don't, be mesmerized into thinking their make-up must be yours. There's a right make-up for you. Find out what it is from an expert. You're alive, not a picture printed on paper!

A real top-of-the-Beauty, Charm, Glamour list and a real must, achievable by anyone, is a properly placed, well-modulated voice. A pleasant voice, which has to include clear enunciation, is not only attractive to those who hear it. The results of its attractiveness are a continually rewarding asset. It is dividend-paying to its possessor. Its appeal is permanent. But the loveliest of faces can only be a briefly appealing mask if an unlovely voice comes from it.

By the turn of a dial, the flick of a switch, the world's most attractive voices enter our homes via television, radio, recordings, motion pictures. Listen to them. Then listen to yourself. Do you speak as you like to be spoken to? Do you speak clearly, authoritatively? Do you speak up and out? If you speak so softly everyone has to strain to hear you, you're a great little tension-provoker to those who must listen. And if you think a personable voice is merely a matter of volume you can create an equally nerve-wracking effect.

If you are one of the gifted people who can learn without any lessons, by all means, teach yourself. But, if you aren't so gifted, lessons will be worth more than gold to you. Voice lessons are not a luxury. An attractive voice isn't a vanity-appeaser. A pleasing voice is a contemporary necessity and worth some sacrifice, if necessary. Budget terms are available for self-improvement courses (at least I know they're available at the studios which present The LORETTA YOUNG Way).

Your hands, your eyes, your thoughts, your voice are beauty facets which you can control, a beauty quartette that can be yours whether or not your face is the most beautiful or the least.

"Isn't she charming?" is a frequent remark about various women. Sometimes we agree, sometimes we don't. The fact is, qualities which charm one person may leave another cold, proving there's no such thing as a charm that will work the same magic on everyone. Perhaps you'll shrug your shoulders, and think, "Why try? What's the use of trying if I can't acquire unfailing charm?" The answer to that is: *your* charm will work its magic widely enough to enrich *you.*

Actually, I don't believe we acquire charm. I think we have to find the real, inherent charm quality that is our very own. I believe everyone has it within himself. I believe we have to find it and I know we have to develop it.

There are certain fundamental qualities, though, without which no one can develop any charm at all.

Selfishness and self-absorption are deadly charm-exterminators. Don't even give charm a thought if you don't give a hoot about pleasing anyone but yourself. We can't charm anyone else by doing only what *we* want to do! The real charm-basic is interest in others. Of which the dividend, payable to you, is: you'll not have time to spend in fretful wonder about whether or not others are interested in giving you "your due." What is really *due* any of us, anyway? Nothing, it seems to me, except what we deserve. Quite selfishly, then, why not work to deserve the best?

I think the first operating rule for charm is the same as the first rule for courtesy, for good manners. Here it is again— The Golden Rule. It works. How it works! Especially when it becomes a habit practiced in one's home, as well as in public!

A charming woman, although she respects other's ideas, beliefs and aspirations, doesn't blindly follow the crowd. She is herself. She makes the most of her own personality, her own appearance.

It doesn't take all the courage in the world to be yourself. You don't have to pretend to possess talents you lack; to have read a book you've never heard of; to have attended an art exhibit or a play or an opera you never saw. Your honest admiration for the talents of others, sincere interest in experiences you've never had, an enthusiastic desire to learn the things about which you're ignorant, will make people remember you as "that woman who was such a fine conversationalist!" Honest! Try it yourself!

A charming woman is a busy woman. She's so interested in the important, exciting things in this busy world of ours that she just hasn't the time for envy, self-pity, petty gossip. And, because she's interested, she's interesting!

I'm sure that you already possess great charm if you possess these good things:

GOOD MANNERS: the practical application of the Golden Rule, doing unto others as we would have others do unto us. The best investment anyone can make anywhere, any time.

GOOD GROOMING: really, consideration for others. Making ourselves attractive to look at and to be with. Grooming doesn't depend on money or physical beauty, but on self-respect, respect for thorough cleanliness, respect for tasteful, correct apparel.

GOOD HUMOR: being of good will, good nature, good disposition; sympathetically responsive to the interests and problems of others, not continually criticizing, belittling, or griping about your own problems. Scattering personal irritabilities all over the place soon destroys being welcome anywhere.

GOOD SENSE: The stabilizing influence which operates as

The Triplets for Everywoman—Beauty, Charm, Glamour

balance, perspective, judgment. Good sense and good taste are twin-friends to us women!

GOOD HABITS: That which we can never "have too much of." It takes determination and energy, to form good habits and more of the same is necessary to practice them in daily life. Good habits demand constant care. But, when they are cared for, they shine so beautifully!

GOOD OUTLOOK: having optimism, enthusiam. Both are the mark of a healthy mind and an affirmative, friendly personality.

Several years ago I did a picture *Half Angel*. It was the story of a girl who walked in her sleep. When she was awake, she was a real Miss Prim 'n' Proper, withdrawn, cold, totally without humor—a real non-glamorous *drip!* But when she wandered around in her sleep, then she was really something! She was relaxed, warm, spontaneous, a delightful, beguiling wit, enthusiastic and glamorous!

I went to a neighborhood theater to see the picture, and when a woman sitting behind me whispered loudly, "How can she look so cold in one scene and so warm in the next?" I was really flattered. I was tempted to turn around and thank that whisperer.

You see, there wasn't any change of costume, nor one bit of difference in make-up. The difference was just a matter of letting my hair down, literally and figuratively when "asleep." I think it proves (at least it does to me) that though outwardly the girl was the same—same make-up, same clothes—in both

221

of her personalities, the difference in her attitude of mind, the quality of her thinking, made her completely drab and unattractive in one state of mind and thoroughly exciting and very attractive in the other.

The point I want to make, if I can, is that it's what's really inside that has to be given as much careful attention as you give to the outer you. No matter how expertly the outer you is served—sleek hair, shadowed eyelids, fashion-wise wardrobe, posture—all these alone can't be added up to the total of beauty, charm and glamour. You don't have a sum at all until your thinking is right on the beam, too. And you can't hire a pilot to get you on it, either. You've got to fly that course yourself.

I don't think glamour is synonymous with sophistication, if that means an obvious, slinky, long-cigarette holder kind of pseudo-sophistication. Unless a girl is clothes-wise she can find herself being totally unglamorous in an ultra-fashionable outfit. Glamour has little to do with wearing just a collection of the latest or the most expensive clothes.

So much for what glamour isn't. One of the things it *is* is taste—the disciplined development of one's instinctive reactions to color and adornment, to the point of knowing exactly how little color and adornment one should use.

Of course, I've gained much knowledge from studio designers. It was Irene who taught me the glamour-importance of planning. If you start with an exciting hat, as I so often do because hats are my weakness, you must restrict yourself to plain shoes, a simple dress, and a minimum of accessories. And, said Irene, "Once you've worked out a perfect combination of bag, hat, jewelry, etc., let well enough alone. The only time you can safely switch accessories is with that sturdy little wardrobe indispensable, your 'basic-black' dress."

Irene also preaches against the common failing of being tempted by an isolated "cute pair of shoes" or a "darling little bag." You buy them (the shoes we'll say) telling yourself they'll go with something. Well, they don't. If you haven't planned an outfit for them, chances are you'll thriftily wear them anyway. And that's just the way you'll look. Anyway.

Edith Head, an indefatigable worker herself, believes personal glamour can be achieved only if you're willing to work at it. She's absolutely right. A few years ago, in one of my bursts of enthusiasm, I bought an organdy dress from a wholesale house. I couldn't return it. And I couldn't wear it. It was just plain blah—as glamorous as a dishrag. After spending an entire afternoon trying it on, taking it off, I finally came up with the brilliant idea of wearing a whole half-dozen starched petticoats under it. Then I fixed up a dreamy green velvet sash for my waist and I wore it that night.

When Cesar Romero took one look at me, walked across the floor and said, "Loretta, tonight I'd like to dance with you," I knew I'd hit the glamour jackpot. But all of my shopping errors weren't so happily corrected. So now I discipline myself as Irene taught me to do.

As an actress I have to be objective about myself. If I don't criticize myself, there are plenty who will do a fine job of it for me! I think all women can afford to be critical of themselves. There are too many things "even your best friend won't tell you!"

I believe a woman should be just as much a perfectionist

about her appearance as she is about the work she does. If she isn't a working girl, she should give the same attention to her appearance as she does to her children's welfare and to her home. Any woman's appearance is part of her welfare.

I've a full-length triple-panel mirror in which I can see every possible angle, and I spend quite a lot of time in front of it because it's an invaluable critic. It's an honest one, too. It reports what it sees. No better, no worse. As a matter of fact, if you asked me, "What is *the* most important material aid to glamour a woman should have?" I'd say, "A triple-panel mirror with good harsh lighting." That mirror gives you the chance to see yourself as others will see you, with your proportions in perspective.

My mirror is an indispensable part of my business, but I think a mirror like that should be indispensable to every woman. She can try on and really check what she wears, and make sure of her "finished" look. Stocking seams straight? Slip showing? Skirt twisted? Hemline even?

It's amazing how much one can learn from that triple-truth-telling mirror—things everyone should know about one's self. There's so much room for improvement in all of us!

I'm sure you know lots of women who never take a real look at their backs. If they did, could they so blissfully wear some of the things we see them in? Skimpy bathing suits, capris or calypso pants? I'm sure they couldn't.

I think that mirror is indispensable as a helper in the first important step—recognition of one's limitations. Face up to them. Then you can learn how to make the best of them. You can't let them get the best of you, can you?

Before I started to learn I made all the mistakes there are. But as I learned, I gained confidence, and as I gained confidence I learned more. It's been very rewarding.

It's so important to look relaxed. To *be* relaxed. Not to feel and look uncertain.

No matter how many of the things we learn of beauty and charm and the last of the triplets, glamour—I believe there's always the danger of being the victim of, well, blind-spots.

I don't think it's safe to count on the legend that "love is blind" and that the man in your life is so blinded that he'll always adore you, whether you're the most glamorous girl in the world or not. Sooner or later, most men exchange courtship's rose-colored glasses for a good sharp magnifying glass. To be safe, it's my suggestion a woman be prepared for that day by using one first!

We've all done dozens of careless things. Little off-beat things in make-up, posture and about our clothes, even in our manners. The fact that most of these digressions are unconscious is what makes them important to all women—and imperative to glamour seekers. And it's what makes me call them beauty blind-spots.

Recently, at Travilla's fashion showing, I noticed a strikingly glamorous young matron. When I looked at her again fifteen minutes later, the entire glamour picture she had created she was now destroying. She was slumped in her chair, shoulders humped forward, her feet and legs wound about one another so that they looked like the distorted limbs of some hoodoo contortionist.

It's not easy to get a detached picture of yourself. But just because it isn't easy doesn't change the fact. It's still exactly what must be done. Look at your face as you look at a stranger —critically, objectively. Wearing more make-up than you should? Or not enough? A friend of mine recently developed a habit of making up her mouth larger. For a while the little extra over-line was becoming. But as weeks went by, she had unconsciously increased the size of her lips until her only rival could be a Ubangi. Anyway, does your lip make-up enhance, or is any resemblance between your mouth and your lip brush's version purely coincidental? Do you wear an over-line which ignores the natural contour? Mouth make-up can be a beauty blind-spot which throws one's entire expression out of line and one's glamour into the ash can.

Mouth and forehead grimaces can do the same thing. A face that is really very lovely in repose can fall apart if, when its owner starts to talk, she distorts every feature. If her mouth puckers up or her forehead wiggles, sending her eyebrows off in opposite directions, her grimaces send her glamour kiting, too. Sadly enough, those who have this blind-spot usually compound their beauty-felony with meaningless hand gestures. Maybe it'll be poking a forefinger into her cheek, pulling at her under-chin—who knows what it'll be! She may be conspicuous but that doesn't mean she's glamorous.

As soon as I get home from a day of work I bathe, brush my hair, put on fresh make-up and slip into a hostess gown. Like charity, I believe glamour should begin at home. There's no law against wanting your family to think you're attractive, too!

Again I say, and definitely; glamour is not insured by a staggering price tag. To prove my point: two of my favorite dresses cost, practically nothing. One is a beige (you can never go wrong buying black, white, grey or beige) wool which has lines as good as any Paris model, even though I found it on the $38.50 rack in the budget department of a Beverly Hills store. Of course, I wear good accessories with it, but it is really a very plain little dress.

My other "prize" is an evening gown I made myself. A long time ago I bought two bolts of imported white silk-net at a close-out sale. (I thought it might make some good curtains some day.) Claudette Colbert invited us to a formal party and I wanted a new dress for it. So I used the whole two bolts of net! I took the underslip of an evening gown, covered the bodice with net, made very narrow shoulder straps, gathered all the rest of the material, yards and yards of it, into a tremendous skirt. Then I wound narrow black velvet ribbon around my waist, fastened it with a huge, real Mystery-gardenia and swept off to the party. I was pretty proud of myself when my gown was called "breathtaking" and I got all sorts of flattering compliments—and until this day I've never told anyone that it wasn't a Werlé original! (I didn't say it *was* a Werlé—I just didn't say it *wasn't*.)

Glamour is something you can't bear to be without, once you're used to it. It isn't something that costs a fortune, but I think glamour comes only after we've made our real investment in learning about beauty and charm and about clothes and fashion. Because after we've learned what we need to know of those things, and are confident of what we know, we're ready to be glamorous. If you're confident, you're comfortable

227

and you're secure in your glamour-judgment. That's what glamour adds up to finally.

I believe, sincerely, that there's beauty and glamour for a woman during every year of her life. There's the bounce and glow of the teenager; the aliveness, vivacity and keen mental interest of the woman in her twenties and thirties. And, if a woman has acquired the tolerance, sympathy and understanding which should result from her experiences in life, I believe mature beauty can be the most enduring of all. Any woman with good taste, good humor and good manners, who possesses and exercises an understanding of the shortcomings of the members of the human race *and* practices the refinements of becoming make-up, hair-style and wardrobe, has a glamour all her own. As glamour should be.

Glamour is ageless. I think a woman can be glamorous at ninety. I know one who is. Even her great-great-granddaughters think she's the *most!*

The split second she ceases to care is the only time a woman ceases to be attractive. If a woman cares about how she looks, and realizes the importance of the beauty of her inner self, she'll make the most of herself inside and out, year in and year out.

Our grandmothers used to say, "Pretty is as pretty does." I've paraphrased it: "Glamour is as glamour cares." Because, if you care about beauty, charm and glamour, you *do* something about them. And what you do will most certainly include what grandma was talking about, too.

And what's wrong about that?

Real feminine. I'll say!

CHAPTER FIFTEEN

Finally—Today!

I DON'T yearn to be a child again, though it's been pleasant to let memory have its way, this once—to review and balance the days that are past. To appraise what I have learned, to see how many of the things I did in the past I would not do today. And, most important of all, to see how much, much more there is for me to learn!

I believe there are particular musts for me because of the absorbing and fascinating business in which I work, and that no must is more realistic than "You must never take yourself too seriously." Of course, my work must be taken seriously, every phase of it, but never my all too-vulnerable self.

The Things I Had to Learn

I believe in living today. Not in yesterday, nor in tomorrow. Nor in wasting one second of the present in regret about the past or worries about the future.

Realizing that yesterday took its "unforgiving minutes" with it into the past makes me zealous about doing my very best with the fast-moving minutes of today, to carry out the obligations which are mine as conscientiously, as kindly, as I possibly can.

I believe in trying to break the too prevalent habit of living as though suspended on an eternal trapeze, swinging widely and wildly between regrets and apprehension. I know a girl who, feeling well and at work, complains continually over even her most routine duties, frets constantly over what will happen to her when she's ill. Of course, she becomes ill (who doesn't, once in awhile?). Then her trapeze whisks her to fretting about what will happen to her wonderful job in her absence. Of course, she recovers. Then she trapezes right back to her gripes and groans about her work and what'll happen when she gets sick again!

She has no present. Her whole life is held captive in a sort of pit between the past and the future. Poor little thing, she's so miserable on her flying trapeze! Wouldn't it be wonderful if she could realize that she can, if she *will*, exercise her right of free choice, leave her trapeze—and land on her feet on the solid terra firma of today?

I believe in the Golden Rule. I believe in practicing it. To treat others as you would have them treat you, really treat them that way, makes this rule the most difficult of all rules to follow all the time, every day. But I know that it can be done, should be done. I believe that practicing the Golden Rule is a habit we should work very earnestly to form. If we do achieve the habit of it, it's all the rule we need to measure our behavior in any human relations. The Golden Rule can take the measure of the very littlest things we do each day. It can take the measure of the way we act or react to great big crises, too. All we have to do with the Golden Rule is *use* it!

I do not hold with those who think it is all right to do whatever you want so long as it doesn't hurt anyone. Who's to be the judge of that? Very few things are without any element of hurt to someone. I believe that if everyone followed every vagrant impulse, in undisciplined indulgence of every selfish desire, chaos exceeding anything imaginable would be inevitable.

I believe you have to nurture your conscience. A conscience has to be given attention the same as any growing thing, if it is to grow strong and helpful to you. The first time you do a wrong thing, your conscience will stir and warn you. If you ignore its warnings, keep repeating the wrong act, the voice of your conscience will grow weaker until you won't hear it at all and no longer think that what you've done is wrong.

But if you listen to your conscience it will grow strong and police your life, and grow and serve you as no other friend you'll ever know.

It's wonderfully pleasant and comforting to be sustained by a good conscience.

I believe in those wonderful words, "To thine own self be true." I don't believe they mean: indulge yourself. I believe they mean: "Be true to the best that's in you." It requires exacting self-discipline to do the things which measure up to one's highest standards. It's unlikely that any human being can achieve perfection—only God is perfect—but we can certainly try our best, keep trying and never stop trying!

I believe that if each and every person really worked to possess self-respect and genuine regard for his fellowman, there could be no crime. There could be no wars. It is possible to prove this—the brotherhood of man under the Fatherhood of God. I believe we should work, trying our best to prove it, every day. I don't expect we'll succeed in measuring up to our intentions every day, but we should be ashamed only if we haven't tried!

At the beginning of World War II a fine young actor placed his whole career—work, money, popularity—on the altar of what he believed. He said, "I want to pick up the wounded on the front line—in advance of the front line. I'll do anything, go anywhere to *help*. But I will not carry a gun. I will not kill."

Our country was at war. Very few cared what he said. He was accused, judged, vilified. Only a handful of even his closest friends recognized how very brave he was and how brave he had to be, to be true to himself.

He offered up as sacrifice, without promise of reward, his career, his fortune, his reputation—all he had. And, in time, his was the great reward. He gave full proof of "thou canst not then be false to any man."

In time, too, his scorners came to envy him because, as men returned from the Pacific Theater, they brought back stories of his tireless, selfless, indomitable courage under fire. Both officers and enlisted men reported he was everywhere—caring for the wounded in the landings and in some of the hottest action in one of our toughest theaters of war. He had had the courage to relinquish material things. He had had the strength of his good conscience. He could speak and act simply, honestly and fearlessly.

Today, Lew Ayres has greater stature than ever before. He stands very tall indeed—true to himself, false to no man.

I remember one night, while the war was still raging, an actor and his wife were discussing him at a dinner party. The man condemned him in a long and bitter harangue until I couldn't keep still any longer.

"I do not know this man at all," I said. "I don't know his mind, his religion, his way of life. They are foreign to me. But I do know he is sincere. To prove what he believes is costing him too much for me to have any doubt of his sincerity. I don't know him. You do. You've known him for years. But, do you know *why* he did what he did? *I* really read his statement. His deep and honest conviction was that no one should kill."

"Well," said the actor, and he was quite belligerent about it, "what kind of a world would this be if everyone in it refused to kill for his country?"

"Why, it would be a dandy world!" I answered. "Just stop and think a moment about what Lew Ayres said, what he gave up everything for, and maybe, before this war ends, he will die for. I know what he said by heart!

" 'In a world where *every* man courageously refused to kill—because of his love of humanity—there could be no war!' "

I believe that if we have lived our lives fully and well, and have accomplished, at least in part, the things which we were put here to do, we will be prepared—mentally, spiritually and physically—for our separation from this world. If we have done our best, we will know the joy of fulfillment, of tolerance and understanding. We'll have the protection of diminished ambition. And whatever has made us afraid of dying will have disappeared.

I know elderly people who have so lived in their long lives. Today they find great pleasure in each and every day. They live easily. They have great composure. They have great serenity. In their great, earned wisdom, they neither rush toward, nor fear, tomorrow. They are content. They have today!

I believe we must resist the opportunities to be very wasteful of simple things, tossing them aside as of no consequence, in a world of almost frenetic concentration on material success.

I don't know many ambition-ridden people who really enjoy themselves. Even success doesn't seem to still the insatiable, gnawing hunger of their ambition. Ambition is a good gift, but it cannot be *all*. It is a gift to cherish only in balance with God's other gifts, whether they are tangible or intangible.

I believe no man is truly successful if his material progress has cost him all the things that money can't buy, and no man is a failure who worships God, loves his country, his home and family, respects himself, his work, his obligations and his fellow-man.

Finally—Today!

I believe that a life without religion is, truly, an impoverished existence. I believe in the efficacy of prayer and have a deep and sorrowful sympathy for one who is without faith. I believe our Father answers *every* prayer—all prayers—with His matchless, inscrutable wisdom, with infinite compassion and with love. I believe in that simple acknowledgment of God's dominion over me and my needs, The Lord's Prayer. I know I must learn and remember *every day* that because He is in all His creatures, there is something to love in everyone, if I'll just remember to look for it. For if I look, I'll find it. And when I talk of sins and shortcomings, it is my own I must be conscious of, not the sins and shortcomings of others.

My most needed help—when I find that what I actually do is far less than the good I aspire to do—lies in knowing that our dear Lord will mercifully judge my inadequacies.

I know I must work earnestly, and every day, to prove these things I believe.

As I am assured that it is the trying that counts, I hope those who chance to read this will do so in charity, realizing that the virtues of which I have written here are those to which I still aspire, and that the faults are those I hope to avoid more and more and until, with continued trying, I finally do erase at least a few of them.

APPENDIX

FACT SHEET

TODAY, Loretta Young is the most Awarded actress in Hollywood.

The Loretta Young Show is television's most Awarded anthology program.

Except for a brace of absences caused by serious illness and normal absence preceding the birth of each of her two sons, Loretta Young has appeared continuously before the cameras since she was twelve years old.

No other Hollywood star has a comparable record. She has been a top Hollywood star since she was fifteen.

As of March 18, 1961, she had 252 performances recorded on film. Eighty-seven in major motion-pictures and 165 in teleplays for *The Loretta Young Show,* not including 300 "Hostess-spots" for The Show.

Two hundred forty-four different characterizations have tested her versatility as an actress and her stamina as a performer.

There is no theater experience, no dramatic-school instruction in her "history."

The lady has really earned her medals!

LORETTA YOUNG—TELEVISION

Since 1953

The Loretta Young Show

NBC-TV

LORETTA YOUNG MOTION PICTURES

1953

It Happens Every Thursday— John Forsythe	U-I

1952

Because of You—Jeff Chandler	U-I
Paula—Kent Smith	Columbia

1951

Half Angel—Joseph Cotten	20th Century-Fox
Cause for Alarm—Barry Sullivan	M-G-M

1950

Key to the City—Clark Gable	M-G-M

1949

*Come to the Stable—John Lund, Celeste Holm	20th Century-Fox
Mother Was a Freshman—Van Johnson	20th Century-Fox
The Accused—Robert Cummings, Wendell Corey	Paramount

*Oscar nomination.

Appendix

1948

Rachel and the Stranger—Robert
  Mitchum, William Holden   RKO

1947

†*The Farmer's Daughter*—Joseph Cotten RKO
The Bishop's Wife—Cary Grant,
  David Niven   Goldwyn-U.A.
The Perfect Marriage—David Niven   Paramount

1946

The Stranger—Orson Welles,
  Edward G. Robinson   RKO

1945

Along Came Jones—Gary Cooper   RKO

1944

And Now Tomorrow—Alan Ladd   Paramount

1943

Ladies Courageous—Phil Terry   Wanger-Universal
China—Alan Ladd   Paramount

1942

A Night to Remember—Brian Aherne   Columbia

  †Oscar received.

1941

Bedtime Story—Frederic March	Columbia
The Men in Her Life—Dean Jagger	Columbia
The Lady from Cheyenne—	
Robert Preston	Universal

1940

The Doctor Takes a Wife—Ray Milland	Columbia
He Stayed for Breakfast—	
Melvyn Douglas	Columbia

1939

Story of Alexander Graham Bell—	
Don Ameche	20th Century-Fox
Wife, Husband and Friend—	
Warner Baxter	20th Century-Fox
Eternally Yours—David Niven	United Artists

1938

Four Men and a Prayer—David Niven	20th Century-Fox
Three Blind Mice—Joel McCrea	20th Century-Fox
Suez—Tyrone Power	20th Century-Fox
Kentucky—Richard Greene	20th Century-Fox

1937

Love Is News—Tyrone Power	20th Century-Fox
Café Metropole—Tyrone Power	20th Century-Fox
Love Under Fire—Don Ameche	20th Century-Fox
Wife, Doctor and Nurse—Warner Baxter	20th Century-Fox
Second Honeymoon—Tyrone Power	20th Century-Fox

Appendix

1936

Private Number—Robert Taylor	20th Century-Fox
Ramona—Don Ameche	20th Century-Fox
Ladies in Love—Tyrone Power	20th Century-Fox
The Unguarded Hour—Franchot Tone	M-G-M

1935

Crusades—Henry Wilcoxson	Paramount
Clive of India—Ronald Colman	20th Century-U.A.
Call of the Wild—Clark Gable	20th Century-U.A.
Shanghai—Charles Boyer	Walter Wanger-U.A.

1934

Born to Be Bad—Cary Grant	20th Century-U.A.
The House of Rothschild—George Arliss	20th Century-U.A.
The Devil to Pay—Ronald Colman	Goldwyn-U.A.
Bulldog Drummond Strikes Back— Ronald Colman	Goldwyn-U.A.
The White Parade—John Boles	Fox Films
Caravan—Charles Boyer	Fox Films

1933

Zoo in Budapest—Gene Raymond	Jesse L. Lasky-Fox
The Devil's in Love—Victor Jory	Fox Films
Heroes for Sale—Richard Barthelmess	Warner Bros.-1st Nat.
She Had to Say Yes—Lyle Talbot	Warner Bros.
The Kid's Last Fight— Douglas Fairbanks, Jr.	Warner Bros.
The Life of Jimmy Dolan— Douglas Fairbanks, Jr.	Warner Bros.

Grand Slam—Paul Lucas	Warner Bros.
A Man's Castle—Spencer Tracy	Columbia
Midnight Mary—Franchot Tone	M-G-M

1932

The Hatchet Man—Edward G. Robinson	Warner Bros.-1st Nat.
Big Business Girl—Frank Albertson	Warner Bros.-1st Nat.
I Like Your Nerve— Douglas Fairbanks, Jr.	Warner Bros.-1st Nat.
Play Girl—Norman Foster	Warner Bros.-1st Nat.
Taxi—James Cagney	Warner Bros.-1st Nat.
Weekend Marriage—Norman Foster	Warner Bros.-1st Nat.
Life Begins—Eric Linden	Warner Bros.-1st Nat.
They Call It Sin—David Manners	Warner Bros.-1st Nat.

1931

The Platinum Blonde—Robert Williams	Columbia
The Ruling Voice—Walter Huston	Warner Bros.-1st Nat.

1930

Devil to Pay—Ronald Coleman	Goldwyn-U.A.
Broken Dishes—Grant Withers	First National
Loose Ankles—Douglas Fairbanks, Jr.	First National
The Right of Way	First National
Road to Paradise—Jack Mulhall	First National
Truth About Youth—David Manners	First National
Man from Blankley's—John Barrymore	Warner Bros.
Second Floor Mystery—Grant Withers	Warner Bros.

Appendix

1929

The Girl in the Glass Cage—Ralph Lewis	First National
Fast Life—Douglas Fairbanks, Jr.	First National
Careless Age—Douglas Fairbanks, Jr.	First National
Scarlet Seas—Richard Barthelmess	First National
The Squall—Carroll Nye	First National
The Forward Pass—Douglas Fairbanks, Jr.	First National
Show of Shows—All Star	Warner Bros.

1928

Laugh, Clown, Laugh—Lon Chaney	M-G-M
Magnificent Flirt—Florence Vidor, Matty Kemp	Paramount

1927

Naughty but Nice—Colleen Moore	First National

AWARDS

LORETTA YOUNG *and* THE LORETTA YOUNG SHOW

TELEVISION ACADEMY OF ARTS AND SCIENCES AWARD—"EMMY"

For:

1959-60—Nominated: "Outstanding Performance by Actress in a Series."

1958-59—*Received: "Best Actress . . . in a Dramatic Series."*

1957-58—Nominated: "Best Continuing Performance (female) Essentially as Oneself."

1956-57—*Received: "Best Dramatic Actress in a Continuing Series."*

1955-56—Nominated: "Best Actress in a Single Performance."

1954-55—*Received: "Best Dramatic Actress in a Regular Series."*

1953-54—Nominated: "Best Female Star of a Regular Series."

MOTION PICTURE ACADEMY OF ARTS AND SCIENCES AWARD—"OSCAR"

1949—Nominated: "Come to the Stable"—20th Century-Fox.

1948—*Received: "The Farmer's Daughter"*—R.K.O.

HOLLYWOOD FOREIGN PRESS ASSOCIATION TELEVISION AWARD—"SILVER GLOBE"

1959—*"For the Consistent Artistry of Her Performances, and the High Quality of Production on The Loretta Young Show."*

Appendix

AMERICAN LEGION AUXILIARY AWARD—"GOLDEN MIKE"—Poll: 1 Million Members

1960—*"Television Program with Greatest Appeal to Women."*

THE NATIONAL EDUCATION ASSOCIATION AWARD— "THE SCHOOL BELL"

(Three Consecutive Years)

1959—*"For Distinguished Service in the Interpretation of Education."*

1958—*"For Distinguished Service in the Interpretation of Education."*

1957—*"For a Distinguished Dramatic Interpretation of Education."*

TV GUIDE AWARD—Readers' Poll (288,000 voters)

1960—*"Most Popular Female Personality."*

HOUR OF ST. FRANCIS AWARD—International Radio & TV Annual Award

1960—*"For Outstanding Service in the Cause of Inspirational TV—to The Loretta Young Show, 1959-60 Season, with Special Recognition of its Production, 'The Road,' and to Loretta Young for Her Performance in the Same Teleplay."*

TV-RADIO MIRROR—"STAR OF THE YEAR"— A Special Award to Loretta Young

1961—*"TV-Radio Mirror is honored to present to Loretta Young this special citation: 'Star of the Year,' for her dedication to high standards in television drama —and for her versatility as an actress."*

THE TV-RADIO MIRROR GOLD MEDAL AWARD—
Readers' Poll

(Six Consecutive Years. Category Was Not in 1960 Poll)

1959—*"Favorite Dramatic Actress on Television."*
1958—*"Favorite Dramatic Actress on Television."*
1957—*"Favorite Dramatic Actress on Television."*
1956—*"Favorite Dramatic Actress on Television."*
1955—*"Favorite Dramatic Actress on Television."*
1954—*"Favorite Dramatic Actress on Television."*

**CANNES FILM FESTIVAL—WORLD TELEVISION—
GRAND PRIX**

(First Grand Prix Awarded to an American Telefilm)

1959—"The Woman Between"—*The Loretta Young Show*

EVERY-WEEK—AMERICAN EDUCATION PUBLICATIONS
International Poll

1959—*"Loretta Young is the Only Star, Male or Female, in
Motion Pictures or Television, Picked by Both Boys
and Girls as Their Favorite in Any Media. From
This Poll, it is Accurate to Describe Her as the
Teenagers' Top-Favorite Television Performer."*

(Every-Week is Current Affairs Newspaper Used in Secondary
Schools Throughout United States and 60 Foreign Countries.)

TEEN-DIGEST SIXTH ANNUAL AWARDS—High School
Editors' Poll

1960—*"Favorite Female Television Personality of 1959."*
(Teen-Digest is Published by Compact Magazine, Inc.,
Subsidiary of the Publishers of Parents Magazine.)

Appendix

COMPACT MAGAZINE NATIONAL AWARD—High School Editors' Poll

(Three Consecutive Years)

1957—*"Best Female Performer on Television."*
1956—*"Best Female Performer on Television."*
1955—*"Best Female Performer on Television."*

THE ROBERT E. SHERWOOD AWARD—Second Prize

1959—*"For The Loretta Young Show, 'The 20¢ Tip,' a Television Program Contributing to the Understanding of Freedom and Justice, Presented by the Fund for the Republic in Memory of Robert E. Sherwood."*

MILLINERY INSTITUTE OF AMERICA AWARD—"Golden Hat"

1961—*"Best Hatted Woman in Television."*
(Poll of Newspaper Editors of the Nation.)
1961—*"One of the Six Best Hatted Women In The World."*
(Poll of two hundred Newspaper Couture experts.)

MOTION PICTURE COSTUMERS AWARD—"FIG LEAF"

1959—*"For the Artistry and Distinction with Which Loretta Young Wears and Interprets Costumes in Her Media."*

BOY SCOUTS OF THE UNITED STATES OF AMERICA AWARD

"In Appreciation of The Loretta Young Show's Service to Boyhood."

GIRL SCOUTS OF THE UNITED STATES OF AMERICA AWARD

> *"The Girl Scout Award for Highest Standard of Program as Well as for Her Interest in the Youth of the Community."*

CALIFORNIA TEACHERS' ASSOCIATION COMMUNICATIONS AWARD (Southern Section)

> 1959—*"For Outstanding Service to Public Education During 1958."*

PHI BETA NATIONAL PROFESSIONAL FRATERNITY— HONORARY MEMBERSHIP

> *"In Conferring Honorary Membership Upon Loretta Young, We Bestow the Highest Compliment in Our Fraternity. In Miss Young, Phi Beta Finds the Perfect Example of the Ideals for Which It Stands. She is an Inspiration to the Aspiring Young Actress . . . and Has Given an Ever Extending Horizon to the Women Seeking a Richer Life."*

STERLING MAGAZINES VICTORIA AWARDS—Readers' Poll—"VIKKI"

(Two Consecutive Years. Only Star to Receive *Four* Awards)

> 1959—*"Best Dramatic Star"*—Adults' Poll.
> *"Best Female TV Star"*—Adults' Poll.
> *"Best Dramatic Star"*—Teenagers' Poll.
> *"Best Female TV Star"*—Teenagers' Poll
> 1958—*"Favorite Female Star"*—Adults' Poll.
> *"Best Dramatic Star"*—Adults' Poll.
> *"Favorite Female Star"*—Teenagers' Poll.
> *"Best Dramatic Star"*—Teenagers' Poll.

DELL PUBLICATIONS' WHO'S WHO IN TELEVISION AWARD—Readers' Poll

1959—*"Best Actress in a Series."*
"Best Female TV Star."

MOTION PICTURE MAGAZINE—Readers' Poll

1960—*"Loretta Young Number Eleven in Both Teenager and Adult Polls Despite Fact That She Had Made No Pictures Since Entering Television."*

LIMELIGHT MAGAZINE 1st ANNUAL AWARD

1960—*"Best Dramatic Actress."*

RADIO AND TELEVISION WOMEN OF SOUTHERN CALIFORNIA AWARD—"GENII"

1957—*"Outstanding Woman in Television—for Her Outstanding Contribution to the World of Communications—and Whose Activities Extend Beyond Her Participation in the Media."*

BEST-DRESSED WOMEN AWARDS (Too Numerous to List)

Loretta Young Is a Long Established Name in This Category.

ST. ANNE'S FOUNDATION—BOARD OF TRUSTEES CITATION

1961—*"This Document of Love and Appreciation is presented to Loretta Young Lewis on Behalf of St. Anne's Maternity Hospital, to Express the Deep Regard in which she is held for her Noble Contribu-*

tions to the Unknown World of The Unwed Mother and Her Baby for the past fifteen years."
(Presented at a Testimonial Reception in honor of Mrs. Tom Lewis.)

SOUTHERN CALIFORNIA FEDERATION OF WOMEN'S CLUBS—A SPECIAL AWARD

1958—*"Television's Outstanding Actress and Program."*

PHI BETA NATIONAL PROFESSIONAL FRATERNITY TELEVISION AWARD

1957—*"The Loretta Young Show."*

AMERICAN INSTITUTE OF VOICE TEACHERS AWARD— Three Years

"Finest Feminine Speaking Voice."

NATIONAL BEAUTY EDITORS' AWARD—"GOLDEN APPLE"

"For the Greatest Contribution as a Female Television Personality in Promoting the General Concept of the Beautiful Woman."

COMMUNITY REHABILITATION INDUSTRIES PRESIDENT'S COMMITTEE AWARD

1959—*"To Loretta Young—Whose Program Has Contributed So Much to Enlightened Human Relations and Whose Portrayals Have Increased Public Awareness of the Problems and Needs of Handicapped Persons."*

Appendix

COMMUNITY REHABILITATION INDUSTRIES AWARD OF MERIT

> 1958—*"Because The Loretta Young Show Has Stressed the Dignity of the Impaired Individual and Elevated the Public Understanding in the Areas of Health, Welfare and Education."*

HOLLYWOOD WOMEN'S PRESS CLUB AWARD— "GOLDEN APPLE"

> *"Most Co-operative Actress."*

WOMAN OF THE YEAR AWARD (S. E. Rykoff Company)

> *"For Her Honest Portrayal of the American Way of Life on The Loretta Young Show."*

THETA PHI ALPHA FRATERNITY AWARD— "The Sienna Medal"

> *"Presented August 20, 1950 to an Outstanding Catholic Woman—Loretta Young."*

SHOW BUSINESS MAGAZINE AWARD

> *"For Artistry and Merit Which Has Enriched the American World of Entertainment."*

BILLBOARD MAGAZINE AWARD

> *"Best Actress in Network Television."*
> *"Best Performer in Any Network Dramatic Program."*

PAN-AMERICAN NATIONS AWARD—"PAN-AMERICAN GIRL"

> *"For Her Popularity in Those Nations"*

FAME MAGAZINE NATIONAL AWARD—TV Editors and Columnists Poll

> *"Best Dramatic Filmed Series."*
> *"Best Dramatic* (Anthology) *Filmed Series."*

LUX RADIO THEATRE—**SPECIAL AWARD**

1951—*"For Loretta Young's twenty-fifth appearance on Lux Radio Theatre, May 21, 1951."*

> (This Award was presented to Loretta Young as the first star to give 25 performances for Lux Radio Theatre. This record was never topped.)

AWARDS ADDENDA

TELEVISION ACADEMY OF ARTS AND SCIENCES AWARD —"EMMY"

Norbert Brodine, A.S.C.

For:
  1957-58—*Received: Best Cinematography.*
  1956-57—Nominated: Best Cinematography.
  1955-56—Nominated: Best Cinematography.
  1954-55—Nominated: Best Cinematography.
      (No Award for Cinematography Prior to 1954)

Richard Morris—Writer-Director

For:
  1957-58—Nominated: *"The Pearl."*

Frank Sylos—Art Director

For:
  1958-59—Nominated: *"Most Honorable Day."*

MOTION PICTURE COSTUMERS' ANNUAL AWARD— "EVE"

Carey Cline—Wardrobe

For: 1959—Nominated: The Loretta Young Show."
  1957—*Received: "The Loretta Young Show."*

The Things I Had to Learn

THE MAKE-UP ARTISTS' ANNUAL AWARD

Otis Malcolm—Make-Up

For: 1957—*Received: "The Pearl"—(Loretta Young's Japanese Make-Up)*.